The Bluegrass Gospel Songbook

by
Wayne Erbsen

NGB-GOS101   NATIVE GROUND BOOKS & MUSIC   ISBN: 978-1-883206-52-9

Thanks!!

Without the help of countless friends, the songs in this book would still be a heap of wadded up scraps of paper in the bottom of my guitar case. My hat's off to Kelli Churchill who transcribed the music and to Laura Boosinger who originally wrote out the music to many of these songs over twenty-five years ago, and to Mr. Bob Willoughby also transcribed a number of the songs. I appreciate proofreading and editing help from Barbara Swell, Mark Wingate, David Currier, Laura Boosinger, Cathy Fink, Marcy Marxer, Hilary Dirlam, Kari Sickenberger, and David Freeman. Thanks to Tina Liza Jones for the guitar illustration, Doyle Lawson for sharing his experiences about bluegrass gospel music, Bruce Nemerov and Lucinda Cockrell for copies of old hymns, the Center for Popular Music to access to their collection of hymn books. Thanks to Mark Freeman and Dave Freeman of Rebel Records for permission to use "I've Just Seen the Rock of Ages." Also thanks to Wayne W. Daniel for information on Charles E. Moody, to Guthrie T. Meade, Dick Spottswood and Douglas S. Meade for their book *Country Music Sources* that was essential in tracking down detailed information about the songs. Thanks also to Tim O'Brien, Ginny Hawker and Glenville State College for information about the songs.

©2006 Native Ground Books & Music. All Rights Reserved
ISBN #978-1-883206-52-9

Contents

Introduction 6

The Roots of Bluegrass Gospel Music 7

Singing the Gospels 11

Painless Gospel Music Theory 13

How to Choose the Right Key 14

Guitar Chords 15

How to Operate a Capo 16

Using the Guitar in Gospel Music 17

Harmony 101 18

Let Your Guitar Teach You Harmony 19

The Dreaded Baritone Part 20

Singing Bass 21

Bluegrass Harmony Singing 22

Amazing Grace in Four-Part Harmony 23

A Beautiful Life 24

A Picture From Life's Other Side 26

Ain't Gonna Lay My Armor Down 28

Amazing Grace 29

Angel Band 30

Are You Washed in the Blood? 31

Beautiful 32

Church in the Wildwood 34

Come and Dine 35

Come Thou Fount 36

Crying Holy Unto My Lord 37

Daniel Prayed 38

Death Is Only a Dream 40

Deep Settled Peace 42

Diamonds in the Rough 44

Don't You Hear Jerusalem Moan? 46

Drifting Too Far From the Shore 48

From Jerusalem to Jericho 50

Give Me the Roses Now 52

Glory-land Way, The 53

Good Old Way, The 54

Grave on a Green Hillside 56

Hallelujah Side, The 58

Hallelujah, We Shall Rise 60

Hand in Hand with Jesus 61

He Will Set Your Fields on Fire 62

Heaven Above 64

Hold Fast to the Right 66

Hold to God's Unchanging Hand 68

Home in That Rock 70

Contents

How Beautiful Heaven Must Be 72

I Am a Pilgrim 74

I Am Bound For the Promised Land 75

I Feel Like Traveling On 76

I Have Found the Way 77

I Heard My Mother Call My Name in Prayer 78

I Will Never Turn Back 80

I Would Not Be Denied 81

If I Could Hear My Mother Pray Again 82

I'll Be No Stranger There 84

I'm Going That Way 86

I'm Going Through 88

I'm S-A-V-E-D 90

In the Garden 92

In the Sweet By And By 94

I've Just Seen the Rock of Ages 95

Jesus, Savior, Pilot Me 96

Just a Closer Walk With Thee 97

Just One Way to the Gate 98

Just Over in the Gloryland 100

Keep on the Sunny Side of Life 101

Kneel at the Cross 102

Leaning on the Everlasting Arms 104

Let the Church Go Rolling On 105

Let the Lower Lights Be Burning 106

Life's Railway to Heaven 107

Little Moses 108

Lone Pilgrim, The 110

Lord I'm Coming Home 111

Methodist Pie 113

My Old Cottage Home 114

Oh! Those Tombs 115

Old Account Was Settled, The 116

Old Gospel Ship, The 118

Old Rugged Cross, The 120

Old-Time Religion 122

On the Sea of Life 124

On the Sunny Side of Life 126

Our Meeting Is Over 127

Palms of Victory 128

Pass Me Not 130

Pilgrim of Sorrow 132

Poor Wayfaring Stranger 133

Power in the Blood 134

Contents

Precious Memories 135
Row Us Over the Tide 136
Royal Telephone, The 137
Shake Hands with Mother Again 138
Shall We Gather at the River? 139
Standing in the Need of Prayer 140
Swing Low Sweet Chariot 142
Take Me in the Lifeboat 144
Take Up Thy Cross 145
Tell Mother I Will Meet Her 146
There Is No Hiding Place Down There 148
Twilight Is Falling 149
Unclouded Day, The 150
Walk in Jerusalem Just Like John 151
Warfare 152
We Are Going Down the Valley 153
We Shall Meet Someday 154
We'll Understand It Better By and By 155
What Would You Give in Exchange? 156
When the Savior Reached Down for Me 159
When They Ring Those Golden Bells 160
When I Laid My Burdens Down 157
When the Roll Is Called Up Yonder 158
Where the Soul Never Dies 161
Where We'll Never Grow Old 162
Who Will Sing For Me? 163
Will the Circle Be Unbroken? 164
Will There Be Any Stars? 165
Won't You Come and Sing For Me? 167
Wondrous Love 166
Working on a Building 168
   Index of Songs 169
   Native Ground Books & Music 172

Western Carolina University

Introduction

If songs are the heart of bluegrass music, then gospel is its soul. For many fans, the bluegrass gospel songs are the most cherished part of a bluegrass performance or recording. It's little wonder that a bluegrass music show is not complete unless it ends with several rousing gospel songs.

This book is the result of a lifelong love of bluegrass gospel music. It actually began in 1983 when I compiled my first gospel songbook that was eventually published in 1993 as *The Old-Time Gospel Songbook*. That book contained fifty-six gospel songs, plus history and stories. This new book contains the songs found in the original book, plus about fifty more. It's been an interesting adventure gathering up these fifty songs. In order to include the very best songs I could find, I had to dance around current copyright laws without stepping on anyone's toes to make sure the songs I included were in the public domain. Don't think for a minute that I didn't try to include more recently copyrighted songs too! I contacted scores of publishers asking for permission. You would have thought I was asking for a loan of a million dollars! Just to use their little song, they wanted my first child, my banjo, my dog and twenty acres of prime farmland. So, if you're thumbing through these pages and are shocked to discover that your favorite gospel song is not included, please don't give up on me. I tried! I really did.

The songs that are included cover a wide spectrum of gospel music. They include ancient hymns, Black spirituals, religious folk songs, songs from the shaped-note tradition, four-part gospel quartets, sentimental religious songs from the late 19th century, camp meeting songs and a few songs from bluegrass song writers who graciously gave me permission to include their songs. Most of the songs are well-known standards of bluegrass gospel music. Some, however, may not yet have been discovered by bluegrass singers. Instead, they've been recorded by old-time country music artists such as Uncle Dave Macon, The Blue Sky Boys, Ernest Stoneman, Gid Tannner and His Skillet Lickers, The Callahan Brothers, and The Carter Family. These are the

Gid Tanner

very same sources that early bluegrass musicians like Bill Monroe and The Stanley Brothers drew from to learn the gospel songs they sang, performed and recorded.

Some of the versions I've printed in the book may be different from what you're used to. That's because whenever possible, I've included the original, or earliest version I could find. Artists who have recorded the songs may have changed (and copyrighted) them along the way. For example, The Carter Family recorded (and changed) "Little Moses." Here at last are the original words and music. I hope you'll find it exhilarating and fun to see what the original song sounded like. Mixed among the well-known songs in the book are some little-known gems. Don't neglect them just because they might be unfamiliar. Even though many of these songs are a hundred years old or more, I promise you, they are tough and will withstand heavy use. My advice is to rear back and sing the bark off of them. They're happiest that way.

The Roots of Bluegrass Gospel Music

Whether you call bluegrass music a revolution started by Bill Monroe or an evolution of old-time country music, gospel songs have been at its heart and soul from the very beginning. Even the earliest rural stringbands from the 1920s learned the secret of warming up an audience with sacred songs. They quickly realized that they could dazzle a crowd with fancy banjo picking and get feet to tapping with lively fiddling, but if they wanted to win the hearts of their audience, they would have to end every program with a rousing gospel song. Even the rowdy Georgia stringband, Gid Tanner and His Skillet Lickers, knew how much their fans loved gospel music. Along with their recordings of down home fiddling and skits about making and drinking moonshine whiskey, members of Gid Tanner and His Skillet Lickers recorded such sacred numbers as "Don't You Hear Jerusalem Moan" and "S-A-V-E-D." Another north Georgia stringband, the Georgia Yellow Hammers, combined such raucous songs as "Going to Raise a Rukus Tonight," "John's Old Grey Mule" and "Fourth of July at a Country Fair" with gospel classic songs they composed such as "Drifting Too Far From The Shore" and "Kneel at the Cross." This winning combination of fiddling, banjo playing, heartfelt singing, and sacred songs certainly helped keep food on the table for many early old-time musicians and those bluegrass performers who followed in their footsteps.

Just as these musicians adapted to changing conditions and musical tastes, so too did gospel songs themselves change and adapt to reflect new influences and inspirations. Many scholars point to the psalms brought over by the early American colonists from the British Isles as the place where gospel music had its deepest roots. In those days, there were so few psalm books that song leaders would "line-out" or "deacon" the words for everyone to follow. Psalms were sung without instruments and were often rendered so painfully slow that one singer remembered, "I myself have twice in one note paused for breath."

By 1734, things began to change when John Wesley published *A Collection of Psalms and Hymns,* which was the first book of religious songs published in the American colonies. Beyond adding to the meager store of psalms that were then in circulation, Wesley's book challenged the notion that psalms were the only legitimate religious songs.

J.E. Mainer's Mountaineers

The Roots of Bluegrass Gospel Music

Once the monopoly of psalms was broken, a wide variety of "folk hymns" were penned, not merely by the clergy, but also by the common people. Drawing their inspiration from the Bible and from earlier hymns, many of these songwriters were convinced that "the devil shouldn't have all the good tunes." They set about composing new religious verses and attaching them to secular melodies that would earlier have been unthinkable. These included such ancient ballads like "Barbara Allen," English fiddle tunes such as "Fisher's Hornpipe," and popular songs from the early to mid nineteenth century such as "Home Sweet Home" and "Darling Nelly Gray." These folk hymns were put in the everyday language of common people and set to familiar and often lively tunes that everyone could sing.

The deep roots of bluegrass gospel songs can also be traced back to the late 1700s when singing-school masters taught a newfangled method of learning music that was called shaped-note singing. Often traveling on horseback or in buggies to rural southern communities, these masters taught countless singers their "shapes." In this method, the notes of the scale were each given a characteristic geometric shape, such as a square or a diamond (see below). With practice, singers who couldn't read standard musical notation could learn to associate the shape of a note with its relative pitch. This enabled entire congregations to sing both the melody and the harmony of new songs in short order. In 1846, Jesse B. Aiden published *The Christian Minstrel*, which went through at least 171 editions and firmly established shaped-note singing as an important factor in the growth and popularity of what would later be called gospel music.

The Roots of Bluegrass Gospel Music

At about the same time that singing-school masters were beginning to teach the rudiments of shaped-note singing in the South, a new type of religious song was born. The first of many camp meetings was held on the banks of the Gasper River in Logan County, Kentucky, in 1800. For several days, entire families traveled by horseback, by wagon, and by foot to hear preachers from as far away as Tennessee or North Carolina. They also came to sing. But the scarcity of hymn books and the wide assortment of denominations, both Black and White, meant that there was no shared body of religious songs that all could sing. This forced song leaders to simplify songs down so that large crowds could easily sing them. It also encouraged the mix of people at the camp meetings to compose new verses right on the spot. The result was soon referred to as "the camp meeting spiritual." In this type of song, a chorus was created where the first line could be repeated up to three times, with only the last line being different. As religious music in America continued to evolve, the harmonies learned through shaped-note singing were combined with the emerging camp meeting spiritual. An example of the camp meeting spiritual is the well-known song, "Give Me That Old-Time Religion."

Give me that old time religion,
Give me that old time religion,
Give me that old time religion,
It's good enough for me.

Dwight Moody & Ira Sankey

Religious leaders have long used songs to unite congregations and fan the flames of religious revival. In 1871, noted evangelist Dwight Moody teamed up with song leader and composer Ira Sankey. Together they barnstormed their way across America's northern cities. In the wake of these revivals, they published a series of books called *Gospel Hymns*. Even though the word "gospel" had been used to refer to religious music as far back as the 17th century, "gospel hymns" came to refer to this more emotional and personal type of religious song. These included the older hymns that were often combined with the verse and chorus patterns that grew out of the camp meeting spiritual. Also included were songs borrowed from Sunday school songsters and YMCA hymn books. Added to these were more contemporary popular compositions by northern songwriters which were often highly personal and deeply sentimental. The degree of success of this combination can be measured by the fifty to seventy million copies that were sold.

The Roots of Bluegrass Gospel Music

With the growing acceptance of the Northern term "Gospel Hymn," Southern religious music began to be called "gospel." Southern gospel drew from its own rich traditions and combined the verse-chorus pattern of camp meeting spirituals with the harmonies learned in southern shaped-note singing schools. By the 1850s, songwriters were composing new gospel songs to appeal to the thousands who flocked to the rapidly growing number of shaped-note singing conventions throughout the south. As shaped-note singers improved their skills, composers were continually challenged to compose new and more intricate songs to keep them coming back to buy more books. The result evolved into new gospel songs that were often attached to popular melodies of the day. These songs combined personal and emotional lyrics with such techniques as call and response, moving parts and bass lead.

Adding fuel to the fire of the growing interest in shaped-note gospel singing, publishers such as James D. Vaughan and Stamps-Baxter began using creative marketing techniques to get more singers to join the ranks of the southern singing conventions. By 1920, Vaughan organized his first gospel quartet, which began touring the singing convention circuit selling songbooks. By the middle of the 1920s, Vaughan had no less than sixteen different gospel quartets on the road selling an estimated half million books a year. In 1922, he started his own record label and the next year he founded his own radio station, WOAN, to give further exposure to his gospel quartets and expand his growing business.

Publishers like Vaughan and Stamps-Baxter relied heavily on their touring quartets to spread gospel music. Stamps-Baxter, for one, hired only singers to work in its publishing house. By day, they printed and published songbooks, and on weekends they formed quartets which sang and sold songbooks at singing conventions and churches throughout the South. Eventually, many members of these quartets became stars in their own right and stepped away from the publishers to establish careers of their own. The songs and styles that were part of this shaped-note singing convention tradition eventually merged with bluegrass instrumental

James D. Vaughan

and vocal styes to create a new genre known as "bluegrass gospel."

Bluegrass musicians who cut their teeth on gospel music in church, at home, or at shaped-note singing conventions, have learned and preserved a large repertoire of these older sentimental shaped-note gospel songs. As early as 1935, J.E. Mainer's Mountainteers began recording gospel quartets in a style identical with the sound that would later be called bluegrass. Musicians such as Bill Monroe, the Stanley Brothers, and Flatt & Scruggs eventually followed suit by making bluegrass gospel music an essential part of each show and recording. Perhaps no other genre of country music has treasured and preserved so many of the old and sentimental shaped-note gospel songs as bluegrass music.

Singing The Gospels

For some people, singing is not an option; it's a requirement. They sing to live and live to sing. Of all the songs in the bluegrass, folk and country repertoire, it is the gospel songs that present the greatest challenge and often give the greatest pleasure. Maybe that's because these songs were created not so much for listening but for singing. For bluegrass singers, the favorite songs have tended to have lyrics that are heartfelt as well as soulful and melodies that are easy to sing on the one hand, and intricate and challenging on the other. For bluegrass gospel singers, perhaps the biggest requirement in selecting a new song is how the song sings in harmony. Whether the song is sung as a duet, a trio, or a quartet, the way the voices come together in harmony is what matters most. Fortunately, The *Bluegrass Gospel Songbook* has well over a hundred great songs to choose from, and each will appeal to any singer, no matter what part they sing.

Bill Monroe

Before we start singing, you might want to familiarize yourself with some common terms that are used in bluegrass music (see box, below). You might also want to understand the difference between bluegrass gospel and Southern gospel. The differences are more a matter of style than content. Both bluegrass and Southern gospel draw from the same repertoire; they both sing out of the same books. In that sense, this book could be called *The Southern Gospel Songbook*.

There are, however, some important distinctions. Bluegrass gospel lead singers are unique in singing songs at the very top of their vocal range. This high pitched singing produces a sound that has been called "the high lonesome sound." We can give Bill Monroe credit for making high singing the standard for bluegrass. Monroe's impact on the vocal range is so strong that if he had been a lighthearted person endowed with a deep voice, we might be calling bluegrass "the low happy sound." But Bill Monroe's role in helping to shape bluegrass and gospel music goes beyond the pitch where songs are sung. Thanks to Bill Monroe, the tenor part in bluegrass has always been a powerful or even dominant part. In fact, on many of Bill's records, his tenor part was so strong that it almost seemed to became the lead itself! It's no wonder that some people have been confused as to the true melody on some Bill Monroe songs.

Lead: The melody or tune.
Tenor: The harmony part right above the lead vocal.
Baritone: The harmony part right below the lead vocal.
High baritone: the part right above the tenor.
Bass: The part below the baritone.

11

Singing The Gospels

Bluegrass gospel harmony is not for the faint of heart. When done right, it should raise the chill bumps on the back of your neck and send shivers all up and down your spine and out into the yard. Just like bluegrass music itself, bluegrass gospel is intense and like a team sport, each singer has a specific job to do.

THE LEAD SINGER generally chooses the song to sing, the key to sing it in, and sets the pace, rhythm and feel of the song. The lead normally sings the melody or tune of the song. Rather than singing in a full, open-throated and relaxed manner that you hear in Southern and Black gospel, bluegrass gospel

Lester Flatt, Earl Scruggs & The Foggy Mountain Boys

singers often tend to tighten their voices and sometimes sing in a slightly pinched or nasal tone. A Southern accent doesn't hurt, either.

THE TENOR is the harmony part just above the lead. Thanks to the legacy of Bill Monroe, the tenor part in bluegrass singing is often so intense it has been called "searing." The tone of the tenor singer should be somewhat biting or sharp. In the South we use the word "keen," like the blade of a knife.

LOW TENOR is sung an octave below the regular tenor part when the lead singer has a high voice.

THE BARITONE normally sings right below the lead and is the most laid back part in a bluegrass gospel quartet. It basically takes whatever part is left over after the lead and tenor find their parts. The distinctive thing about the baritone is that it is not distinctive. Instead, the baritone's tone should be rather bland or mellow so as not to detract from the character of the lead singer's voice. In some ways the baritone serves as the glue that binds the entire harmony together.

HIGH BARITONE the baritone part that is sung above the tenor, instead of below it.

THE BASS is the lowest part in the gospel quartet. The bass singer's tone should be deep and full and he normally sings the root of the chord.

NOTE: In general, bluegrass vocals are without vibrato. Occasionally the lead vocal can use a little vibrato, but no other part normally uses it.

When you are learning to sing harmony, there's no substitute for doing a lot of listening. You should steep yourself in the gospel harmony of groups such as Mainer's Mountaineers, Bill Monroe and the Bluegrass Boys, The Stanley Brothers, Flatt & Scruggs, Jim and Jesse, Carl Story, and Doyle Lawson. Listen to the vocal part that matches your vocal range and try to stay on that part without straying over to the next part.

Painless Gospel Music Theory

Don't let the word "theory" scare you. I promise to explain this to you as painlessly as possible. Relax. At the top of every page of music in *The Bluegrass Gospel Songbook*, it will tell you the "key" of the song. "Amazing Grace," for example, is in the key of G. What does that mean? The "key" tells you what scale will be used on a particular song and what chords to play.

A "scale" consists of the notes you'll use to sing a song. A song in the key of A, for example, would use an A scale. For singing the songs, you don't have to be concerned with the scale. In fact, forget I even mentioned it! You WILL, however, need to know about chords if you're going to accompany yourself on the guitar, piano, autoharp, banjo, mandolin, dulcimer, and even the fiddle. A "chord" is a group of at least three notes that are in harmony with each other. The chords will be shown above the lines of music in the book. The good news is that only three chords will be needed to play most gospel songs. For your convenience, we've given them Roman numerals to identify these three chords: I, IV and V. They are circled on the top of the chart, above.

Key	(I)	II	(IV)	(V)	VI
A	A	B	D	E	F#m
B	B	C#	E	F#	G#m
C	C	D	F	G	Am
D	D	E	G	A	Bm
E	E	F#	A	B	C#m
F	F	G	B♭	C	Dm
G	G	A	C	D	Em

Using "A Beautiful Life" (page 24) as an example, you can see that the chords for that song are A, D and E. If you look at the top of the chart above, you'll see for the key of A, the "I" chord is A, the "IV" chord is D, and the "V" chord is E. If "A Beautiful Life" is too low for your voice to sing in the key of A, no problem. Merely go UP the alphabet and try it in the key of C, D, or E. The chart above will tell you what chords to substitute. If you try the key of C, for example, the "I" will be C, the "IV" will be F, and the "V" will be G.

The songs in the book are arranged alphabetically and each song is in a key that should be comfortable for a male with a mid-range voice. The keys were also chosen to be easy to play on most stringed instruments. If you are a female or a male with a very high or low voice, feel free to change the key of any song to suit your voice or instrument.

How to Choose the Right Key

It's essential to sing a song in the right key for your voice. If you're singing with other people, you may have to pitch the song so it works for everyone, including the tenor and bass singers. Sometimes that takes some doing! How do you determine what is the right key? If you are a male with an average voice, you should first try to sing the songs in the keys that are written in the book. Begin by strumming the chords on your favorite stringed instrument and singing the melody by reading the music, or get a music-reading friend to pick out the melody for you on their instrument of

It doesn't matter if your voice is high, low, or in the middle; don't hesitate to change the key of the songs in this book. Generally, women sing about a fourth higher than men. That would mean that a song that is written in the key of G for an average male voice would be sung in the key of C by a woman with an average range. Using the illustration below,

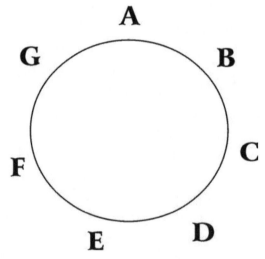

choice. If the song is too low, merely go UP the musical alphabet and pick a new key (and set of chords) that is higher in pitch. Consulting the handy illustration above, UP means you would go clockwise around the circle. The letters (A, B, C, etc.) represent the key. Once you've selected a new key to try, look at the chart at the top of page 13 to see what chords to play in the new key.

start with G and count four letters clockwise around the circle to C. You can also consult the handy chart below. Keep in mind that finding the right key is NOT an exact science, but something that is often done by trial and error and even blind luck. Once you identify a great key to sing a song in, be sure to make a note of it for the next time you sing it.

Key of an average male singer.	G	A	C	D	E	F
Key of an average female singer.	C	D	F	G	A	B♭

Guitar Chords

For singing bluegrass gospel songs, the guitar is essential. If you haven't yet learned to play the guitar, now might be the right time. Below are pictured the common guitar chords you'll need to play most of the songs in this book. Tip: When you're first learning the chords, be sure to make your fingers go to each chord *ALL AT THE SAME TIME*, rather than one-finger-at-a-time.

To read the chord chart below, the six lines represent the strings on your guitar and the black dots tell you where to put your fingertips. The string on the far right side is the first or littlest string, and the sixth or fattest string is on the left.

The basic guitar chords needed to play every song in this book are shown below. Beneath each chord are two numbers, which represent your bass strings. The bass strings are the two strings that you alternate between in a "tick-tock" fashion. After each bass string, you would play a single crisp downward strum over the bottom three or four strings of your guitar with a flat pick. The bass strings played with the strum should sound like "boom chuck," "boom chuck." You will notice that each song in the book has the chords to the song written on top of the staff. Stay on that chord until a new chord is called for. NOTE: Don't play the strings marked with an "X."

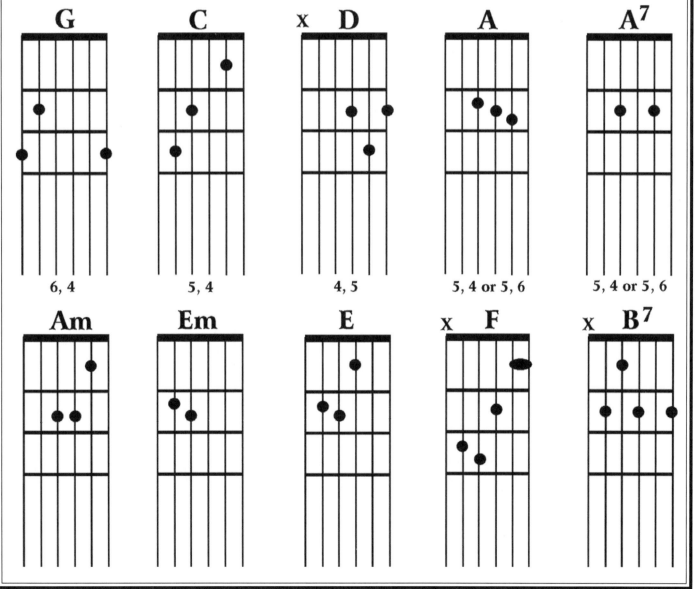

15

How to Operate a Capo

As you sing your way through this book, you'll frequently want to sing the songs in keys other than the ones they are written in. On page 14 we talked about the I, IV, and V and the secret of substituting one set of chords for another. Beyond that, you'll sometimes find it necessary to use a capo, which is a device which clamps on the fingerboard of a guitar or banjo and raises the pitch and changes the key. Using a capo is easy and your capo will be your new best friend. I suggest purchasing a capo that will stay ON the instrument when not in use, rather than one that you can forget where you left it last.

There are several ways to use a capo. If a song is a little too low to sing in the key in the book, try putting the capo on the second fret, use the same chords, and see if that's a better key to sing the song. If it's still too low, move it up another fret or two until the key feels comfortable for your voice. By the way, the fifth fret is normally as high as you want to go your capo, unless you don't mind if your guitar sounds like a plastic wind-up toy!

Slapping the capo on a random fret and trying the hit or miss method is certainly one way to find the best key in which to sing a song. If you prefer a slightly more scientific approach, below is a useful chart to help you manage your capo.

Let's say a song is in the key of G but is too low for your voice. Look at the chart below and find the G in the column on the left. The numbers along the top represent the spaces between the metal frets on your guitar or banjo. If you put your capo on the second fret, your G magically becomes an A. This means that you're fingering a G chord but it sounds like an A. Likewise, if you put your capo all the way up on the 5th fret and play a G chord, it will sound like a C chord. In this case, rather than fool with the capo, which will sometimes cause your strings to rattle and buzz and get out of tune, I suggest you go back to the chart on page 14 and just play your I, IV and V chords for the key of C, which would be C, F and G.

Frets

Chord	1	2	3	4	5
G		A	B$^\flat$	B	C
A	B$^\flat$	B	C		D
C		D		E	F
D		E	F		G
E	F		G		A

Capo Chart

Using The Guitar in Gospel Music

Your trusty guitar is the perfect instrument to play while singing. Even more important than its role as an accompanying instrument, the guitar can also help teach you to sing harmony. As we'll soon learn, singing in harmony is nothing more than singing chords. What are "chords?" A chord is three or more notes that sound good when played or sung together. They sound "harmonious." The guitar is the ultimate chordal instrument, so it makes sense that the guitar can help you learn to sing chords. NOTE: don't play or sing the strings marked with an "X."

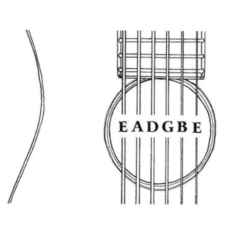

EADGBE

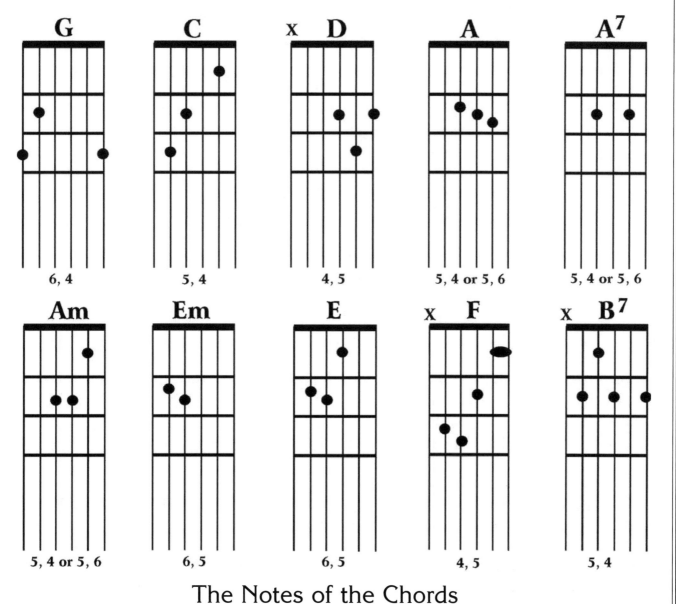

The Notes of the Chords

Harmony 101

Before we can learn to sing harmony, we need to know a wee bit of music theory. This won't hurt (much), I promise. The musical alphabet that is used by musicians and singers alike is made up of notes that are named A, B, C, D, E, F and G. After some of the notes there is a #, which stands for "sharp." "Sharp" means one half step higher in pitch. The easy way to know where the sharps belong is to remember that there are no sharps between B and C and between E and F. This means there is no B# and no E#. Take a look at this illustration of the musical alphabet. As you go clockwise around the circle, you're getting higher in pitch, and vice versa.

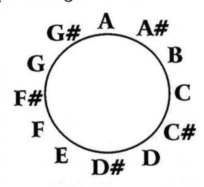

Armed with this knowledge, you can now understand how harmony works. When you're singing harmony, you're singing chords. A chord is normally made up of just three notes: the root, the third, and the fifth. The root is easy to figure out because it has the same name as the chord. The root of a G chord is a G, and so on. To figure out the third of any chord, start at the root and count FOUR places around the circle. To get the fifth, count SEVEN places around the circle. For example, if you want to know the notes of a D chord, the D would be the root. Counting four slots clockwise from D would be F#. To get the fifth, count seven slots from D and you get A. Now try it for yourself with another note as your root. If you hate to figure out this kind of stuff and want the answers presented on a silver platter, the chart to the right is that platter.

Assuming you've learned a few guitar chords, set your guitar on your lap and slowly strum a G chord with your right thumb or pick. As you can tell from the chart at the bottom, the three notes of a G chord are G, B and D. Don't let the fact that there are six strings on the guitar confuse you. There are still only three notes in a G chord: the one or root (G), the third (B), and the fifth (D). Remember that the first string is the one closest to the floor. Here are the names and numbers of the G chord: 1-G, 2-B, 3-G, 4-D, 5-B, 6-G. NOTE: The three notes of each chord are shown under each guitar chord on the previous page. By the way, seventh chords, such as A7 or B7, are the exception, and have four notes.

Let's try singing some harmony. Play the third string from the floor, the G note. As you are playing that G, sing that note. The next harmony note higher in pitch from the root of G is the third, which is the B. On the guitar, that's the second string played open. Sing the B. Finally, the next higher harmony note of the G chord is the fifth, or D. Here, you would fret the second string at the third fret to get the D. Sing the D. Practice singing those three notes of the G chord, starting with the lowest note: G, B, and D. To help you find those notes, you can play them on the guitar and match your voice to them. Practice moving from one harmony note to another.

Chord	Root	Third	Fifth
A	A	C#	E
B	B	D#	F#
C	C	E	G
D	D	F#	A
E	E	G#	B
F	F	A	C
G	G	B	D

The Notes That Make a Chord

Let Your Guitar Teach You Harmony

After you've worked a bit on singing the three notes of several chords, it's time to bring in your singing buddy to learn to sing harmony together. For now, one singing partner is probably plenty. You need to learn to sing two-part harmony before you learn to sing in a trio or a quartet.

Begin by strumming a chord on the guitar. How about a C? The chart on page 18 will tell you that the three notes of a C chord are C, E, and G. Referring to the guitar chart on page 17, you'll see that when you hold down a C chord, the C notes can be found on the fifth string and the second string. The E notes will be on the fourth string at the second fret, the first string played open and the sixth string played open. The G note is the third string open. If you want a higher G note, you can play the first string fretted at the third fret. Decide between yourselves which of you is going to sing lead and who will try the tenor harmony. You can take turns. Normally, the singer with the lower voice will sing lead and the one with the higher voice will sing the tenor.

Now, play a little game. The lead singer sings one of the three notes of the chord, and the tenor singer will sing the next higher harmony note. For the C chord, for example, if the lead sings a C, the tenor would sing the E above that C in pitch. If the lead sings the E, the tenor would sing the G, and so on. Take turns singing lead and harmony. Don't forget to double check your harmony notes by playing the lead and tenor notes on the guitar that you find on the chart on the opposite page.

Once you've practiced singing some harmony notes with your singing partner, it's time to try your skills on a gospel song. Let's give "Amazing Grace" a shot. Like most songs, "Amazing Grace" has just three guitar chords. In this case, which is the key of G, the chords are G, C, and D. While on each of those chords, the lead vocal will be singing ONLY the three notes of the chord: G, B, and D. The three notes of the C chord are C, E, and G, and the three notes of the D chord are D, F#, and A. For each note the lead singer sings, the tenor singer will find the next higher note of the chord. Having your guitar on your lap will help. The melody of "Amazing Grace" starts with a D, which is the fourth string played open on the guitar. The tenor would sing the next higher note of the G chord, which is a G, which is the third string played open on the guitar.

Let's summarize. There are at least two ways to figure out the tenor part for yourself. 1) Consulting the chart on page 18 will tell you that the three notes in a G chord are G, B, and D. Strum a G chord on your guitar and look at the G chord on the guitar chart on the opposite page. Your ear should tell you that the next higher note from a G is a B, the second string open. 2) OK. Your ears failed you. What next? The circle chart on page 18 is your next source of wisdom. As you go clockwise around the circle, the notes get higher in pitch. So the next highest harmony note of a G will be the B, and so on. As the lead singer slowly sings each melody note of "Amazing Grace," the tenor will sing the next higher note of the chord.

The Dreaded Baritone Part

I jokingly titled this page "The Dreaded Baritone Part" because the baritone is the most feared, misunderstood and, by the way, most fun part to sing. Curiously, the baritone is the most mild-mannered and meekest part of a quartet, so there's nothing to be afraid of. The baritone's job on the team is to sing the third note of the chord. It basically gets "leftovers." In plain English, that means it gets whatever note is left over after the lead and tenor have each grabbed their part.

Think of harmony singing like a sandwich. A duet would be your basic open-faced sandwich, with the lead singer being the bread and the tenor being the baloney or cheese on top. A trio would be like a regular closed-faced sandwich, where the lead singer becomes the meat or cheese in the middle, the tenor is the piece of bread on top, and the baritone would be the bottom piece of bread. Now chew on that for a while!

When you're learning to sing baritone, gather your two favorite singers around you and play the harmony game. Have somebody strum a G chord on the guitar and remember that the three notes of a G chord are G, B, and D. The lead gets to go first, singing one of the notes of the chord. Let's say he or she sings a B (second string on the guitar played open). The tenor then sings the next higher note of the chord, the D (second string played at the third fret). What note of the chord is left? G. The baritone gets the G (third string played open on the guitar). After you've tried all the various combinations of the G chord, try the game with the other chords in the key of G, which are C or D. If you can't quite find the notes by ear, check with the chart on the bottom of page 18.

HIGH BARITONE: Although the baritone normally sings below the lead, in some cases, the baritone singer sings the third note of the chord above the tenor. This part is called "high baritone." We use this technique when the lead singer pitches a song too low for the baritone singer to reach with any comfort. In this case, the baritone singer would sing the third note of the chord above the tenor.

When singing the regular baritone part, you have to be concerned with more than just filling in the third note of the chord. We're talking about "tone." While the lead vocalist should sound strong and full of character and the tenor voice should be high and piercing, the baritone should sound rather bland. Your job as a regular baritone singer should be to let the lead, tenor and bass parts shine. You need to be almost invisible but still audible. Your note should be heard but should not stand out. Instead, it should be somewhat understated. Note: because the high baritone part is often pitched so high, it can't help but sound piercing, so if you're singing that part, go ahead and let 'er rip.

Photo by Michael Wilson

Doyle Lawson

Singing Bass

Curiously, in bluegrass music the bass part is only used on the gospel songs. In secular songs, you commonly hear solos, duets and trios but seldom do you hear quartets. The only exception was in the 'sixties when Lester Flatt would amble up to the mic and announce that the whole band would gang around to sing the next song, which could either be sacred or secular.

Earl Scruggs, Jake Turlock, Paul Warren & Lester Flatt

Luckily for bass singers, they play an active and essential role in bluegrass gospel music. Unlike secular bluegrass, in bluegrass gospel, the bass singer frequently sings the lead part, albeit briefly. Examples of songs in this book that feature bass lead are "A Beautiful Life," "Daniel Prayed," and "He Will Set Your Fields on Fire." Songs with bass lead are certainly some of the most exciting pieces of music in bluegrass gospel.

The bass singer's main job in a gospel quartet is to sing the root of each chord. On a G chord, for example, the root is a G, and so on. Since there are normally just three notes in a given chord, it's obvious that in a four-part gospel song, two of the singers are often singing the same note. As you might guess, the "dirty " job of doubling someone else's note falls on none other than the long-suffering bass singer.

When you are learning to sing bass, my best advice on singing bass is to strap on the headphones and do a lot of listening. There's no shortage of bluegrass gospel recordings to listen to. I suggest you steep yourself in the early recordings of the master himself, Bill Monroe. Knowing who sang bass on Monroe's many gospel recordings is tricky, because he had so many singers and they changed from session to session. Strangely, on the Monroe Brothers recording session of August 3, 1937, Bill himself sang bass on "He Will Set Your Fields on Fire." On some of Monroe's gospel recordings in the early 'fifties, his brother Birch sang bass. In the mid to late 'fiftes, the bass singing was done by Milton Estes, William D. Killian, and Gordon Terry, although fiddler Bobby Hicks often sang bass in live shows during this period. In the 'sixties and early 'seventies, a studio musician named Culley Holt sang bass on the recordings of the Bluegrass Quartet.

Art Wooten, Bill Monroe, Cleo Davis & Amos Garren

Bluegrass Harmony Singing

Bluegrass gospel is all about harmony. The rich mix of duets, trios and quartets heard on recordings and live shows makes for some incredible listening. But the greatest pleasure of all is singing the harmonies with other singers. As good as the songs in this book are, to really get their full flavor, you have to sing them in harmony.

Of course, there are many ways to learn to sing harmony. Many old-timers have regaled me with stories of learning to sing shaped-note harmony in church. Just this past week, I spoke with 85-year-old Jack Shelton, who recorded gospel songs with Wade Mainer in the early 'forties, and I also spoke with Doyle Lawson, who has one of the finest bluegrass gospel groups performing today. Both these men confirmed that they learned shaped-notes in church. But recently, while calling Wade Mainer to wish him a happy 99th birthday, Wade told me he never read the shapes. Instead, he learned all the melodies and harmonies by ear. Another of Wade Mainer's old musical sidekicks, Zeke Morris (author of "Salty Dog Blues"), once told me he learned gospel music by sneaking in the back door of Black churches to learn their style of gospel singing.

All this is to say that there's no one "right" way to learn to sing harmony. In this book the melodies are printed in standard "round notes," not shaped-notes, so any musical instrument can play these songs. If you don't read music and don't know anyone who does, here's a musical staff showing the most common musical notes along with the name of each note. This may help you decipher the music in the book.

To sound out the melodies in the book, it might be useful to play them on the guitar. For your convenience, here is the guitar fingerboard with the notes provided for you. Keep in mind that for any given song you will only need a few of these notes, so don't be overwhelmed by all these notes! For example, in the key of G there are normally just three chords: G, C, and D. Each of these chords contains three notes: G chord - G, B, and D; C chord - C, E and G; D chord - D, F#, A. So, if you're picking out a song on the guitar, you'll need just nine notes or so. That's it!

To help you visualize how harmonies work, "Amazing Grace" is written out in four part harmony on page 23. For each melody note of the song, the four harmonies (lead, tenor, baritone, and bass) take turns singing the three notes that make up each chord. Remember that the tenor will be the next note of the chord higher than the lead. The baritone is just below the lead, and the bass, of course, is down in the basement, singing the root of the chord.

Amazing Grace in Four Part Harmony

Guitar	G						C		G
Tenor	G	B	D	B	D	D	C	G	G
Lead	D	G	B	G	B	A	G	E	D
Baritone	B	D	G	D	G	D	E	C	B
Bass	G	G	G		G	G	C	G	G

A - maz - ing grace how sweet the sound

Guitar							D
Tenor	G	B	D	B	D	D	F#
Lead	D	G	B	G	B	A	D
Baritone	B	D	G	D	G	G	A
Bass	G	G	G		G	B	D

That saved a wretch like me

Guitar		G				C		G
Tenor	D	G D	G D	B	G	C	G	G
Lead	B	D B	D B	G	D E	G	E	D
Baritone	G	B G	B G	D	B	E	C	B
Bass	D	G	G	G	G	C	G	G

I once was lost but now am found

Guitar					D		G
Tenor	G	B	D	B	D	C	B
Lead	D	G	B	G	B	A	G
Baritone	B	D	G	D	F#	F#	D
Bass	G	G	G		D	D	G

Was blind but now I see.

A Beautiful Life

William M. Golden   Key of A   William M. Golden

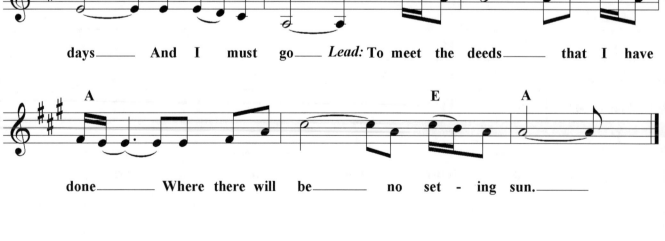

Each day I'll do_____ a gold - en deed_____ By help - ing

those_____ who are in need._____ My life on earth_____ is but a

span_____ And so I'll do_____ the best I can._____

Chorus

Bass: Life's ev - 'ning sun_____ is sink-ing low_____ a few more

days_____ And I must go___ *Lead:* To meet the deeds_____ that I have

done_____ Where there will be_____ no set - ing sun._____

A Beautiful Life

Byron Parker & His Mountaineers

The words and music of "A Beautiful Life" were composed by William M. Golden in 1918. It was first recorded by Smith's Sacred Singers on April 5, 1927, but the North Georgia Four called it "Each Day I'll Do A Golden Deed" for their July, 1928 recording. The third group to record it was the Vaughan Quartet on May 20, 1930. Other quartets who have waxed "A Beautiful Life" include The Chuck Wagon Gang (11/25/36), The Monroe Brothers (1/28/38), Wade Mainer & Sons of the Mountaineers (9/26/38), and Byron Parker & His Mountaineers (2/9/40). "A Beautiful Life" features a bass lead on the first two lines of the chorus.

Each day I'll do a golden deed
By helping those who are in need.
My life on earth is but a span
And so I'll do the best I can.

    Life's evening sun is sinking low
    A few more days and I must go
    To meet the deeds that I have done
    Where there will be no setting sun.

To be a child of God each day
My light must shine along the way.
I'll sing His praise while ages roll
And strive to help some troubled soul. (Chorus)

The only life that will endure
Is one that's kind and good and pure.
And so for God I'll take my stand
Each day I'll lend a helping hand. (Chorus)

I'll help some one in time of need
And journey on with rapid speed
I'll help the sick, the poor and weak
And words of kindness to them speak. (Chorus)

While going down life's weary road
I'll try to lift some traveler's load.
I'll try to turn the night to day
Make flowers bloom along the way. (Chorus)

A Picture from Life's Other Side

Charles E. Baer   Key of G   Charles E. Baer

The Blue Sky Boys

Although not strictly a gospel song, "A Picture from Life's Other Side" was popular with many gospel singers in the 'twenties and 'thirties. It was one of two songs that Smith's Sacred Singers sang when they first auditioned in a makeshift studio in Atlanta's Kimble House Hotel for Columbia Records on April 22, 1926. Because these early recordings could only hold about three minutes of music, the group was forced to leave off the last verse, which is included here. The song was composed by Charles E. Baer in 1896. It was apparently edited or arranged by Georgia composer John W. Vaughan, who included it in his 1900 songbook, *Windows of Heaven, No 8*. In the 'twenties it was recorded by Vernon Dalhart, and The Jenkins Sacred Singers. In the 'thirties it was made popular by Bradley Kincaid and recorded by Smith's Sacred Singers (again), and covered in the 'forties by The Blue Sky Boys. Since then, it's been recorded by a rather eclectic group of musicians that includes Hank Williams, Ramblin' Jack Elliott, Woody Guthrie, Cisco Houston, George Jones, Jerry Lee Lewis, Mac Wiseman, and Hank Williams Jr. Note that the verse and the chorus have the same melody.

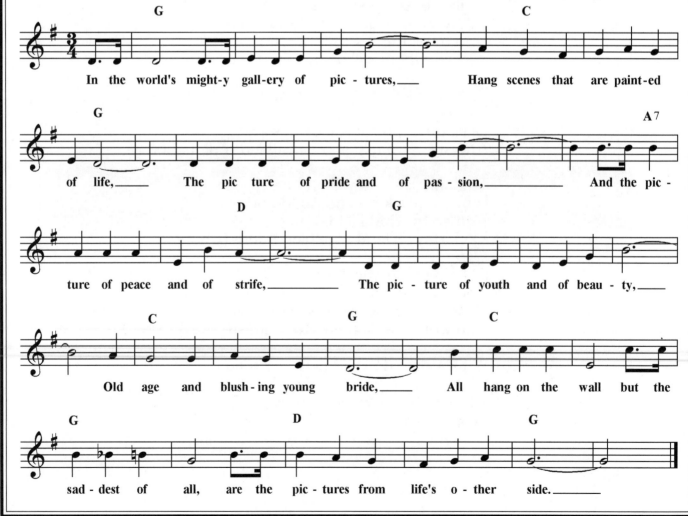

In the world's might-y gall-ery of pic - tures,____ Hang scenes that are paint-ed of life,____ The pic ture of pride and of pas - sion,____ And the pic - ture of peace and of strife,____ The pic - ture of youth and of beau - ty,____ Old age and blush - ing young bride,____ All hang on the wall but the sad - dest of all, are the pic - tures from life's o - ther side.____

A Picture from Life's Other Side

In the world's mighty gallery of pictures,
Hang the scenes that are painted of life,
The picture of pride and of passion
And the picture of peace and of strife,
The picture of youth and of beauty,
Old age and a blushing young bride,
All hang on the wall, but the saddest of all,
Are the pictures from life's other side.

'Tis a picture from life's other side,
Somebody has fell by the way
A life has gone out with the tide,
That might have been happy some day.
Some poor old mother at home,
Watching and waiting alone,
Longing to hear from a loved one so dear,
'Tis a picture from life's other side.

The first scene is that of a gambler,
Who lost all his money at play,
Takes his dead mother's ring from his finger,
That she wore on her wedding day,
His last earthly treasure he stakes it
Bows his head that his shame he might hide
When they lifted his head, they found he was dead,
'Tis a picture from life's other side. (Chorus)

The next was a scene of two brothers,
Whose paths in life differently led,
The one was in luxury living,
The other one begged for his bread,
Then one night they met on the highway,
"Your money or your life" the thief cried,
He then with his knife took his own brother's life,
'Tis a picture from life's other side. (Chorus)

The last is a scene of a river,
Of a heartbroken mother and babe,
In the harbor light glare stands a shiver,
An outcast that no one will save,
And yet she was once a true woman,
She was somebody's darling and bride,
God help her she leaps, there's no one to weep,
'Tis a picture from life's other side. (Chorus)

Photo by Wayne Erbsen

Ain't Gonna Lay My Armor Down

Key of G

This song by an unknown composer smacks of camp meeting or brush arbor days when songs were sung without hymn books by the light of a pine knot torch. These kinds of songs had to be so simple that virtually anyone could follow them. "Ain't Gonna Lay My Armor Down" was first recorded by McVay and Johnson in Johnson City, Tennessee, on October 18, 1928. The Kentucky Coon Hunters recorded it on June 17, 1931. It's been done bluegrass style by Jim Mills.

Chorus

Ain't gonna lay my ar - mor down, Ain't gonna lay my ar - mor down, Ain't gonna lay my ar - mor down 'til He comes, Ain't gonna lay my ar - mor down, Ain't gonna lay my ar - mor down, Ain't gonna lay my ar - mor down 'til He comes.

I'm gonna sing and shout and pray,
I'm gonna sing and shout and pray,
I'm gonna sing and shout and pray 'til He comes,
I'm gonna sing and shout and pray,
I'm gonna sing and shout and pray,
I'm gonna sing and shout and pray 'til He comes.

Ain't gonna run when the battle gets hot,
Ain't gonna run when the battle gets hot,
Ain't gonna run when the battle gets hot, 'til He comes,
Ain't gonna run when the battle gets hot,
Ain't gonna run when the battle gets hot,
Ain't gonna run when the battle gets hot, 'til He comes.

Amazing Grace

John Newton Key of G Anonymous folk melody

No hymn can rival "Amazing Grace" for its universal popularity and appeal. The composer of the lyrics was John Newton, who was born in England in 1725. At the age of nine his mother died and he was shipped off to sea as a cabin boy. He later deserted the British navy but was whipped and put in irons. Rising through the ranks, he eventually became captain of a slave ship. During a violent storm Newton found solace in God and he later left the sea and became an ordained minister of the Church of England. After composing the lyrics to "Amazing Grace" in 1789, Newton set the words to an anonymous hymn tune that often appears in old hymn books as "New Britain" or "Harmony Grove."

A - maz - ing_____ grace how sweet the

sound That saved a____ wretch like me._____ I

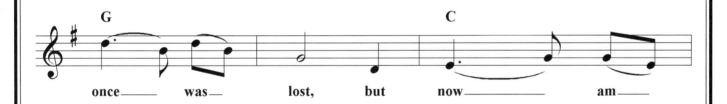

once_____ was____ lost, but now_____ am____

found, was blind but____ now I see._____

'Twas grace that taught my heart to fear
And grace my fears relieved.
How precious did that grace appear
The hour I first believed. (Chorus)

Through many dangers, toils and snares
I have already come.
'Twas grace that brought me safe thus far
And grace will lead me home. (Chorus)

When we've been there ten thousand years
Bright shining as the sun.
We've no less days to sing God's praise
Than when we first begun. (Chorus)

Angel Band

Jefferson Hascall   Key of G   William Batchelder Bradbury

Although its original title was "My Latest Sun is Sinking Fast," this hymn has also been published under the title "The Land of Beulah." It was composed in 1860 by Jefferson Hascall and William Bradbury and it first appeared in J.D. Dadmun's *Melodian.* Born in York, Maine, on October 6, 1816, Bradbury became an organist, piano teacher and singing-school master as well as a prolific composer and compiler of sacred books. His nine hundred hymns and fifty-nine books sold more than two million copies. "Angel Band" was first recorded by Smith's Sacred Singers on April 17, 1928 in Atlanta, Georgia. It acquired new fame when The Stanley Brothers' 1955 recording for Mercury was played during the closing credits of the 2000 film, *O Brother, Where Art Thou?*

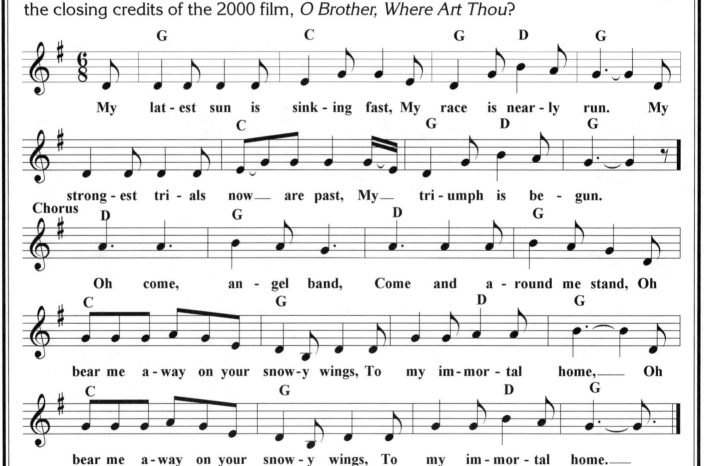

My lat-est sun is sink-ing fast, My race is near-ly run. My

strong-est tri-als now— are past, My— tri-umph is be-gun.

Chorus

Oh come, an-gel band, Come and a-round me stand, Oh

bear me a-way on your snow-y wings, To my im-mor-tal home,— Oh

bear me a-way on your snow-y wings, To my im-mor-tal home.—

I know I'm nearing the holy ranks
Of friends and kindred dear
For I brush the dews on Jordan's banks
The crossing must be near. (Chorus)

I've almost gained my heavenly home
My spirit loudly sings
Thy holy ones, behold they come!
I hear the noise of wings. (Chorus)

Oh bear my longing heart to Him
Who bled and died for me
Whose blood now cleanses from all sin
And gives me victory. (Chorus)

Are You Washed in the Blood? 1878

Rev. E.A. Hoffman   Key of A   Rev. E. A. Hoffman

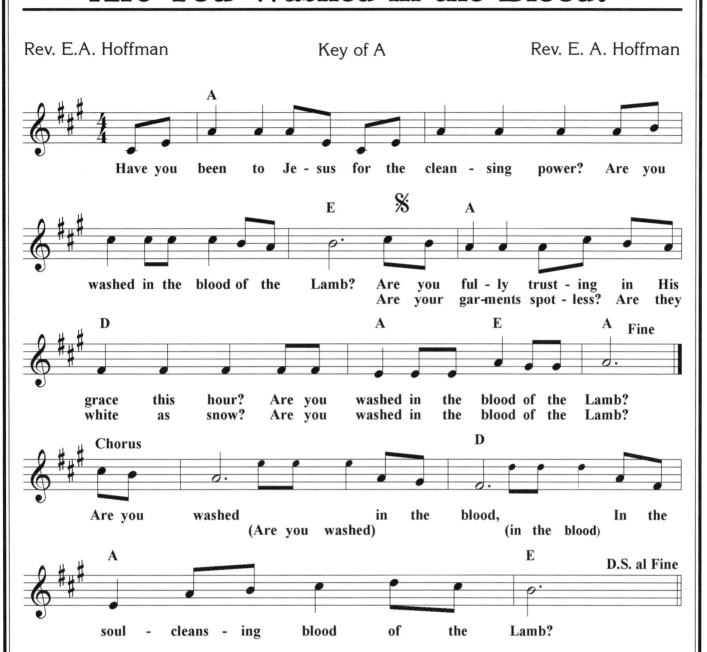

Have you been to Je-sus for the clean-sing power? Are you washed in the blood of the Lamb? Are you ful-ly trust-ing in His grace this hour? Are you washed in the blood of the Lamb?

Are your gar-ments spot-less? Are they white as snow? Are you washed in the blood of the Lamb?

Chorus

Are you washed in the blood, In the (Are you washed) (in the blood)

soul-cleans-ing blood of the Lamb?

Are you walking daily by the Savior's side?
Are you washed in the blood of the Lamb?
Do you rest each moment in the Crucified?
Are you washed in the blood of the Lamb? (Chorus)

When the Bridegroom cometh will your robes be white?
Are you washed in the blood of the Lamb?
Will your soul be ready for the mansion bright?
Are you washed in the blood of the Lamb? (Chorus)

Lay aside the garments that are stained with sin
And be washed in the blood of the Lamb,
There's a fountain flowing for the soul unclean
Oh, be washed in the blood of the Lamb. (Chorus)

Beautiful

B.E. Warren   Key of A   B.E. Warren

Beau - ti - ful robes so white, Beau-ti-ful - land of light, Beau-ti-ful

home so bright, Where there shall come no night; Beau-ti-ful crown I'll wear,

Shin-ing with stars o'er there, Yon-der in man-sions fair, Gath-er us there.

Chorus

Beau-ti-ful robes   Beau-ti-ful land,
Beau - ti - ful robes of white,   Beau - ti - ful land of light,

Beau-ti-ful home   Beau-ti-ful band,
Beau-ti - ful home so bright,   Beau - ti - ful band of might

Beau - ti-ful crown,   Shining so fair,
Beau - ti-ful, Beau - ti-ful crown, Shin-ing, yes, shin-ing so fair

Beau-ti-ful man - - - sion bright, Gath-er us there.
Beau - ti - ful man - sion bright   yes, gath - er us there.

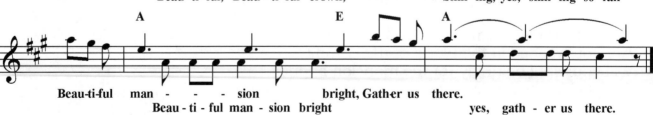

32

Beautiful

This lovely hymn lives up to its title beautifully. It was first published in A.J. Showalter's 1904 book *Best Gospel Songs & Their Composers* with the words and music by B.E. Warren. It was a favorite of The Blue Sky Boys, who recorded it for Starday Records. The overlapping words on the chorus make this an ideal song to sing in a group setting.

Beautiful robes so white, beautiful land of light,
Beautiful home so bright, where there shall come no night;
Beautiful crown I'll wear, shining with stars o'er there,
Yonder in mansions fair, gather us there. (Chorus)

Beautiful robes,
     (Beautiful robes of white,)
Beautiful land,
     (Beautiful land of light,)
Beautiful home,
     (Beautiful home so bright,)
Beautiful band,
     (Beautiful band of might,)
Beautiful crown,
     (Beautiful, beautiful crown
Shining so fair,
     (Shining, yes, shining so fair,)
Beautiful mansion bright,
     (Beautiful mansion bright,
Gather us there.
     (Yes, gather us there.)

Beautiful thoughts to me, we shall forever be,
Thine in eternity when from this world we're free;
Free from its toil and care, heavenly joys to share,
Let me cross over there, this is my prayer. (Chorus)

Beautiful things on high, over in yonder sky,
Thus I shall leave this shore, counting my treasures o'er,
Where we shall never die, carry me by and by,
Never to sorrow more, heavenly store. (Chorus)

"He could pray a whole bowl of mashed potatoes cold just asking the blessing."

Church in the Wildwood

William S. Pitts   Key of G   William S. Pitts

In 1855 the Congregational Church in Bradford, Iowa had no church building, so the members met in a store, an abandoned school house, and even in a lawyer's office. A twenty-seven year-old medical student named William S. Pitts was visiting the area and envisioned a church in a grove of trees, which he called "the little brown church in the vale." Returning to his home in McGregor, Iowa, Pitt soon composed the lyrics and music to "The Church in the Wildwood." When news of the song reached Bradford, the church's new minister, Rev. John K. Nutting, encouraged his congregation to build a church using volunteer labor and donated funds. This song became the only known song to inspire the building of a church.

There's a church in the val-ley by the wild - wood, No
love - li - er spot in the dale, No—— place is so dear to my
                      No   spot is so dear to my
child - hood as the lit - tle brown church in the vale.
child - hood as the lit - tle brown church in the vale.

Chorus
Come to the church in the wild-wood, Oh, come to the church in the vale,

Oh, come to the church in the wildwood
To the trees where the wild flowers bloom,
Where the parting hymn will be chanted
We will weep by the side of the tomb. (Chorus)

From the church in the valley of the wildwood
When day fades away into night,
I would fain from this spot of my childhood
Wing my way to the mansions of light. (Chorus)

How sweet on a clear Sabbath morning
To list to the clear ringing bell,
Its tones so sweetly are calling
Oh, come to the church in the vale. (Chorus)

Come And Dine

C.B. Widmeyer   Key of C   C.B. Widmeyer

A favorite song of Grandpa Jones, which he recorded in 1975 on *16 Sacred Gospel Songs* (King 822). C.B. Widmeyer wrote the words and music in 1907.

Je - sus has a ta - ble spread, Where the saints of God are fed,
With His man-na He doth feed, And sup - plies our ev - 'ry need;

He in - vites His chos - en peo - ple "Come and dine,"
O, 'tis sweet to sup with Je - sus all the time!

Chorus

"Come and dine," the Mast - er call - eth, "Come and dine;" You may
(O, come and dine)

feast at Je-sus' ta - ble all the time; He who fed the mul - ti - tude, Turned the
(O, come and dine)

wa - ter in - to wine, To the hun - gry call - eth now, "Come and dine."

The disciples came to land, thus obeying Christ's command,
For the Master called to them, "Come, come and dine;"
There they found their hearts' desire, bread and fish upon the fire,
Thus He satisfies the hungry ev'ry time. (Chorus)

Soon the Lamb will take His bride to be ever at His side,
All the host of heaven will assembled be;
O, 'twill be a glorious sight, all the saints in spotless white;
And with Jesus they will feast eternally. (Chorus)

Grandpa Jones

Come Thou Fount

Rev. Robert Robinson, 1758   Key of G

Only a few hymns can boast such a long and intricate history as "Come Thou Fount." Its complete title is "Come Thou Fount of Every Blessing," but it has also been published and recorded under the title "I Will Arise," and also "Olney." The chord structure of the song fools you into thinking it is in the key of C, but it is actually arranged here in the key of G. Scholars disagree on the exact origin of the melody, but most affirm it originated in the British Isles. Annabel Morris Buchanan found evidence that "Come Thou Fount" descended from the Scottish tune "Hynde Horne," which dates back to the 13th century or earlier. Guthrie Meade calls it a Welsh tune named "Hyfrydol" from 1835 and gives credit to Francis Frederick Chopin and possibly John Wyeth. American folk hymn scholar George Pullen Jackson has found pieces of the melody of "Come Thou Fount" in such hymns as "Humble Penitent," "Hayden," "Bozrah" and "New Orleans." The lyrics of "Come Thou Fount" were written in 1758 by Rev. Robert Robinson (1735-1790). As a young man growing up in England, he had been a ruffian and a hooligan, but he changed his rowdy ways when he was seventeen after attending a religious service by the evangelist George Whitehead. He wrote the lyrics to "Come Thou Fount" only six years later.

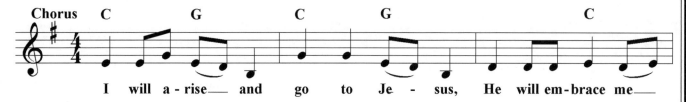

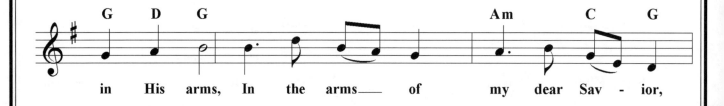

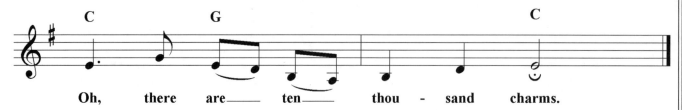

Come thou fount of every blessing,
Tune my heart to sing Thy grace,
Streams of mercy never ceasing,
Call for songs of loudest praise. (Chorus)

Teach me some melodious sonnet,
Sung by flaming tongues above,
Praise the mount, I'm fixed upon it,
Mount of Thy redeeming love. (Chorus)

Here I'll raise my Ebenezer,
Hither by Thy grace I'm come,
And I hope by Thy good pleasure,
Safely to arrive at home. (Chorus)

Jesus sought me as a stranger,
Wandering from the fold of God,
He, to rescue me from danger,
Interposed His precious blood. (Chorus)

Crying Holy Unto My Lord

Key of G

The Carter Family called this song "On the Rock Where Moses Stood" when they recorded it in Memphis, Tennessee, on November 24, 1930, but the song can be traced to Black sources much earlier. Bill Monroe recorded it in Atlanta, Georgia, October 7, 1940, but Monroe's version is identical to that of Wade Mainer & The Sons of The Mountaineers, who recorded it on February 4, 1939.

Chorus

Cry - ing hol - - y un - to my Lord, Cry - ing

hol - y un - to Lord, Oh, if I___ could I

sure - ly___ would stand on that rock, Lord, Lord, where Mos - es stood.

Sinners, run (sinner, run) and hide your face (and hide your face),
Sinners, run (sinner, run) and hide your face (and hide your face),
Go run unto the rocks and hide your face
For I ain't (Lord, Lord) no stranger now. (Chorus)

Lord, I ain't (Lord, I ain't) no stranger now (no stranger now),
Lord, I ain't (Lord, I ain't) no stranger now (no stranger now),
I been introduced to the Father and the Son
And I ain't (Lord, Lord) no stranger now. (Chorus)

Jack Shelton, Tiny Dotson, Wade Mainer & Howard Dixon at WWNC

Daniel Prayed

Daniel Prayed

GT. Speer   Key of G   G.T. Speer

I heard about a man one day who wasted not his time away
He prayed to God every morning, noon and night;
He cared not for the king's decree, but trusted God to set him free,
Old Daniel prayed, every morning, noon and night.

    Old Daniel served the living God, while here upon this earth he trod,
    He prayed to God, every morning noon and night;
    He cared not for the things of Baal, but trusted One who never fails,
    Old Daniel prayed every morning, noon and night.

They cast him in the lion's den, because he would not honor men,
He prayed to God every morning, noon and night;
Their jaws were locked, it made him shout, and God soon brought him safely out,
Old Daniel prayed every morning, noon and night. (Chorus)

Oh, brother, let us watch and pray, like Daniel, live from day to day,
Old Daniel prayed every morning, noon and night;
We, too, can gladly dare and do the things of God, He'll take us through,
Old Daniel prayed every morning, noon and night. (Chorus)

Speer Family

"Daniel Prayed" is among the most challenging and fun gospel songs to sing. It was composed in 1936 by George Thomas Speer, who was better known as G.T. "Dad" Speer. Born in Fayetteville, Georgia, in 1891, G.T. was raised on a farm near Houston, Alabama. G.T. always loved to sing, and by the age of seventeen, he was studying music with several local teachers. Although G.T. often sang in church and taught singing-school, he did most of his singing while plowing behind his two mules, Kate and Beck. On a hot summer day in 1923, G.T. was plowing his fields when he broke his plow and decided right then that he'd rather be making music than plowing. Selling his farm, he moved his family to town to pursue the music business full time with his group, the Speer Quartet. Needing a car to travel to churches and singing conventions, the Speers scraped together the $475 it took to purchase a shiny new Model A Ford. By 1930, the Speer family had moved to be near family in Lawrenceburg, Tennessee, where G.T. got a job working for an insurance company while singing part time. As luck would have it, Lawrenceburg was the home of James D. Vaughan, and before long G.T. was hired by Vaughan to teach music and promote Vaughan's songbooks. The Speers later joined forces with the Stamps-Baxter company, which helped to promote the Speer Quartet's radio career on WSFA in Montgomery, Alabama. For the Speers, radio was the key that led to commercial success on records and gospel performances. They have been called "America's First Family of Gospel Music."

Death is Only a Dream

Rev. C.W. Ray   Key of G   A.J. Buchanan

In the early 1890s Rev. C.W. Ray wrote the lyrics and A.J. Buchanan composed the tune of "Death is Only a Dream." In 1892 the hymn was copyrighted by R.M. McIntosh. Three years later it appeared in David E. Dortch's book, *Gospel Voices*, published in Nashville, Tennessee. This book credits H.B. Ponder for composing the lyrics. The first group to record it was The Paramount Sacred Four, who waxed it in September of 1927. Among the groups who recorded it was The Jenkins Family. The patriarch of the group, Andrew Jenkins, was a blind Holiness preacher, musician, former newsboy, and constant composer. The more than eight hundred songs he composed include "God Put a Rainbow in the Clouds," "Dream of the Miner's Child," "Ben Dewberry's Final Run," and "The Death of Floyd Collins."

Sad - ly we sing, and with trem - u - lous breath, As we

stand by the my - sti - cal stream,___ In the val - ley and by the dark

riv - er of death And yet 'tis no more than a dream.

Chorus
On - ly a dream, on - ly a dream, And glo - ry be - yond the dark stream,___ How

peace-ful the slum-ber, How hap-py the wak-ing for death___ is on - ly a dream.

Death is Only a Dream

Sadly we sing, and with tremulous breath,
As we stand by the mystical steam,
In the valley and by the dark river of death,
And yet 'tis no more than a dream.

Only a dream, only a dream,
And glory beyond the dark stream,
How peaceful the slumber, how happy the waking,
For death is only a dream.

Why should we weep when the weary ones rest,
In the bosom of Jesus supreme,
In the mansions of glory prepared for the blest?
For death is no more than a dream. (Chorus)

Naught in the river the saints should appall,
Though it frightfully dismal may seem,
In the arms of their Savior no ill can befall,
They find it no more than a dream. (Chorus)

Over the turbid and onrushing tide,
Doth the light of eternity gleam,
And the ransomed the darkness and storm shall outride,
To wake with glad smiles from their dream. (Chorus)

Hank Williams once said that "Death Is Only a Dream" was his favorite song.

Deep Settled Peace

Kate Sturgill Peters   Key of D   Kate Sturgill Peters

I found no rest for my soul Till I

heard_____ the sto-ry told, Now I'm in_____ the Shep-herd's

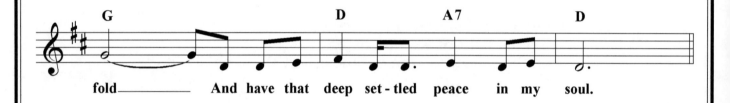

fold_____ And have that deep set-tled peace in my soul.

Chorus

There's a deep set-tled peace in my soul._____ I've been re-

deemed and made whole, I've been washed in the blood of the Lamb And I

know I un-der-stand, That deep set-tled peace in my soul._____

Deep Settled Peace

Kate Peters was moved to compose "Deep Settled Peace" while sitting at her father's bedside just before he passed away in 1928. One of thirteen children, Kate grew up in coal mining country near Norton, Virginia. Even by the age of seven she showed a keen interest in music and was soon playing the parlor organ and later the guitar. In her teens she joined with her brothers and formed a string band. Kate was distantly related to A.P. Carter, of the famous Carter Family, who lived not far away in Maces Springs, Virginia. A.P. was constantly collecting songs in neighboring counties and he frequently took Kate along as kind of a "walking tape recorder." While A.P. busily copied down the words from the singers he met, Kate would memorize the melodies. She would later sing them back to A.P., Sarah and Maybelle so they could learn the songs.

In addition to helping A.P. Carter's song collecting efforts, Kate had an active music career on her own. In the late 'twenties, she teamed up with a group of her Wise County neighbors and formed The Lonesome Pine Trailers. She later formed a musical partnership called The Cumberland Valley Girls with a young lady with the unlikely name of Meadie Moles.

"Deep Settled Peace," although not widely known, is surely a classic gospel song. Those who have recorded it include The Phipps Family, John McCutcheon, and Ginny Hawker & Kay Justice.

I found no rest for my soul,
Till I heard the story told,
Now I'm in the Shepherd's fold,
And have that deep settled peace in my soul.

   There's a deep settled peace in my soul,
   I've been redeemed and made whole,
   I've been washed in the blood of the Lamb,
   And I know I understand,
   That deep settled peace in my soul.

Let not your heart be troubled so,
If to Jesus you will go
And of Him you'll learn to know,
You'll have that deep settled peace in your soul. (Chorus)

Then when death around you lies,
And you must cross the Great Divide,
If you have Jesus on your side,
There'll be a deep settled peace in your soul. (Chorus)

"That's where you get your mail, fan letters, you know, is from the sacred. I don't care how hot a number you got out, you won't get the mail on it like you will on the sacred numbers." Lester Flatt June 17, 1972

Diamonds in the Rough

C.W. Byron   Key of G   L.L. Pickett

Uncle Dave Macon

On September 9, 1926 Uncle Dave Macon positioned himself in front of a single microphone in the Vocalion studio in New York City and recorded "Diamonds in the Rough." The words had been written by C.W. Byron and the melody by L.L. Pickett and copyrighted in Pickett's book *Tears and Triumphs* in 1897. It was the Carter Family's February 15, 1929 recording of "Diamonds in the Rough" that helped spread its popularity far and wide. Since then, it's been recorded by the likes of Johnny Cash, John Prine, Merle Travis, The Nitty Gritty Dirt Band and Norman Blake. To my knowledge, no one has yet to record all the verses. Here, at last, is the entire song, six verses plus the chorus.

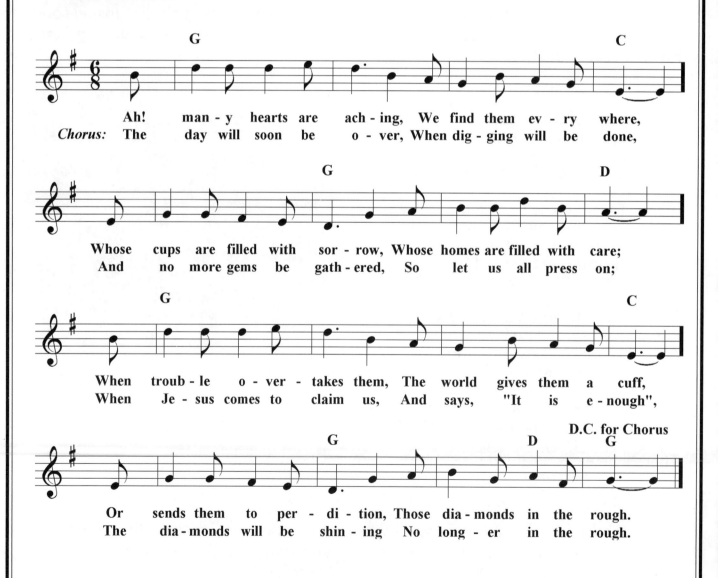

Ah!   man - y hearts are   ach - ing, We find them ev - ry   where,
Chorus: The   day will soon be   o - ver, When dig - ging will be   done,

Whose   cups are filled with   sor - row, Whose homes are filled with   care;
And   no more gems be   gath - ered, So   let us all press   on;

When   troub - le o - ver - takes them, The world gives them a   cuff,
When   Je - sus comes to   claim us, And says, "It is e - nough",

Or   sends them to per - di - tion, Those dia - monds in the rough.
The   dia - monds will be shin - ing No long - er in the rough.

D.C. for Chorus

Diamonds in the Rough

Ah! many hearts are aching, we find them everywhere,
Whose cups are filled with sorrow, whose homes are filled with care
When troubles overtakes them, the world gives them a cuff
Or sends them to perdition, those diamonds in the rough.

    The day will soon be over when digging will be done,
    And no more gems be gathered, so let us all press on;
    When Jesus comes to claim us, and says, "It is enough,"
    The diamonds will be shining no longer in the rough.

One day, my precious comrades, you, too, were lost in sin,
When someone sought your rescue, and Jesus took you in;
So when you're tried and tempted by the scoffers' keen rebuff,
Remember, O remember, they're diamonds in the rough. (Chorus)

O there are many diamonds long buried in the earth,
We pass them by unnoticed, but Jesus knows their worth;
He bids us seek and find them, His message is enough,
He'll save and sanctify them, these diamonds in the rough. (Chorus)

There are complaining people who say we are too bold,
And then there are still others who say we're after gold;
But they are all mistaken, we crave no earthly stuff,
But souls of poor lost sinners, those diamonds in the rough. (Chorus)

While reading through the Bible, some wondrous sights we see,
We read of Peter, James and John, by the sea of Galilee;
And when the Master called them, their work was rude enough,
Yet they were precious diamonds He gathered in the rough. (Chorus)

Now keep your lamps a-burning, the lamps of perfect love,
And unto every sinner point out the way above;
The precious blood of Jesus was shed, and that's enough,
Oh, let us tell them of it, those diamonds in the rough. (Chorus)

Don't You Hear Jerusalem Moan?

Key of G

Well, the Meth-od-ist preach-er, you can tell him where he go; Don't you

hear Je-ru-sa-lem moan? Don't____ nev-er let a chick-en get

big e-nough to crow; Don't you hear Je-ru-sa-lem moan? *Chorus* Don't you

hear Je-ru-sa-lem moan? Don't you hear Je-ru-sa-lem

moan? Thank God there's a heav-en been a-ring-ing in my soul, And my soul's got

free,____ Don't you hear Je-ru-sa-lem____ moan?____

Don't You Hear Jerusalem Moan?

This playful novelty song has been poking fun at religion since it first appeared in *The American Songster* published in Philadelphia by W.A. Leary in 1845. The product of the playful imagination of an unknown minstrel-era songsmith, "Don't You Hear Jerusalem Moan?" was a regular part of the stage show of many blackfaced minstrels in the 1840s. These colorful performers did their best to appease rowdy audiences while decked out in ill-fitting patchwork clothing and over-sized shoes. In those rough and tumble early stage shows, theater-goers were not easily impressed. Many came to shows armed with baskets of rotten fruit and vegetables which they routinely hurled at unwitting performers who did not suitably entertain them. Little wonder "Don't You Hear Jerusalem Moan?" has lasted for over one hundred and fifty years. It was and still is a crowd pleaser! Among the first musicians trying to capitalize on this novelty song was Gid Tanner & His Skillet Lickers whose April 17, 1926 recording is faithfully transcribed here.

> Well, a Methodist preacher, you can tell him where he go,
> Don't you hear Jerusalem moan?
> Don't never let a chicken get big enough to crow,
> Don't you hear Jerusalem moan.
>
> > Don't you hear Jerusalem moan?
> > Don't you hear Jerusalem moan? Thank God
> > There's a heaven been a-ringing in my soul and my soul's got free,
> > Don't you hear Jerusalem moan?
>
> Well, a hard-shell preacher, you can tell him how he do,
> Don't you hear Jerusalem moan?
> Well, he chews his own 'bacco and he drinks his own brew,
> Don't you hear Jerusalem moan? (Chorus)
>
> Well, the Baptist preacher you can tell him by his coat,
> Don't you hear Jerusalem moan?
> Has a bottle in his pocket that he can't hardly tote,
> Don't you hear Jerusalem moan? (Chorus)
>
> Well, the Campbellite preacher, his soul is saved,
> Don't you hear Jerusalem moan?
> Well, he has to be baptized every other day,
> Don't you hear Jerusalem moan? (Chorus)
>
> Well, the Holy Roller preacher sure am a sight,
> Don't you hear Jerusalem moan?
> We'll he gets 'em all a-rolling and he kicks out the light,
> Don't you hear Jerusalem moan? (Chorus)
>
> Well, the Presbyterian preacher, he lives in town,
> Don't you hear Jerusalem moan?
> Neck's so stiff he can hardly look around,
> Don't you hear Jerusalem moan? (Chorus)

Drifting Too Far From the Shore

Charles W. Moody   Key of G   Charles W. Moody

Out on the per - il - ous deep, Where dan - gers si - lent - ly creep,

And storms so vi' - lent - ly sweep, you are

drift - ing too far from the shore. Drift - ing too far from the shore, from the shore.

you are drift - ing too far from the shore, Come to Je - sus to - day, Let Him
peace - ful shore.

show you the way, you are drift - ing too far from the shore.

Drifting Too Far From the Shore

Charles W. Moody had a way not just with words, but with composing melodies too. Besides "Drifting Too Far From the Shore," which he wrote in 1923, he also composed the gospel classic "Kneel at the Cross." Although his heart and soul was in gospel music, he was also the unlikely source for "Song of the Doodle Bug," which he recorded with his band, The Georgia Yellow Hammers.

The list of artists who have recorded "Drifting Too Far From the Shore" reads like a Who's Who of bluegrass and early country gospel. Curiously, Charles W. Moody himself never got the chance to record it. First to commit the song to a record were the Carolina Gospel Singers on September 27, 1929, in Richmond, Indiana, for the Gennett label. Those who followed suit includes The Monroe Brothers, Porter Wagner, Hank Williams, Carl Story, Jerry Garcia, Boone Creek, Pure Prairie League, Old & In the Way, Tennessee Ernie Ford, Bill Monroe, Rose Maddox, the Country Gentlemen, Roy Acuff, Red Smiley, Don Stover, The Stanley Brothers and Emmylou Harris, as well as Helen, June and Anita Carter.

Out on the perilous deep,
Where dangers silently creep,
And storms so violently sweep,
You are drifting too far from the shore.

Drifting too far from the shore,
You are drifting too far from the shore (peaceful shore),
Come to Jesus today, let Him show you the way,
You are drifting too far from the shore.

Today the tempest rolls high,
And the clouds overshadow the sky,
Sure death is hovering nigh,
You are drifting too far from the shore. (Chorus)

Why meet a terrible fate,
Mercies abundantly wait,
Turn back before it's too late,
You are drifting too far from the shore. (Chorus)

Photo by Blanton Owen

Garden Creek Baptist Church, Allegheny/Wilkes County line, NC

From Jerusalem to Jericho

Rev. W.M. Robinson   Key of D   Rev. W.M. Robinson

From Je ru sa lem to Jer i co, a long that lone ly road,

A cer tain man was sat up on and robbed of all his load.

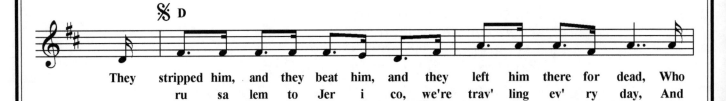

They stripped him, and they beat him, and they left him there for dead, Who
ru sa lem to Jer i co, we're trav' ling ev' ry day, And

was it, then, that came a long and bathed his ach ing head?
ma ny are the fall en ones that lie a long the way.

Tell me who, _____ tell me who, _____ Tell me,
tell me who, yes, who,

who was his neigh bor, kind and true? _____ From Je -
so kind and true.

50

From Jerusalem to Jericho

In the early days of the recording industry, the Gar-ner Brothers were the first to record "From Jerusa-lem to Jericho" in Richmond, Indiana on Novem-ber 1, 1924. Uncle Dave Macon, "The Dixie Dewdrop," loved this gospel song so much he recorded it twice. The first time was for Vocalion on April 14, 1925 in New York City. In Charlotte, North Carolina, on August 3, 1937, he recorded it again, with the song appearing on Bluebird and Montgomery Ward, both budget labels.

Uncle Dave Macon

The song itself was composed by Rev. W.M. Robinson in 1891. The first known printing of the song was in *Apostolic Hymns, A Collection of Hymns & Tunes* published in Fulton, Kentucky, in 1898.

From Jerusalem to Jericho along that lonely road,
A certain man was sat upon and robbed of all his load.
They stripped him, and they beat him, and they left him there for dead,
Who was it, then, that came along and bathed his aching head?

   Tell me who, tell me who,
   Tell me who was his neighbor kind and true?
   From Jerusalem to Jericho we're trav'ling ev'ry day,
   And many are the fallen ones that lie along the way.

From Jerusalem to Jericho a certain priest came by,
He heard the poor man calling, but he heeded not his cry,
He drew his robes about him then and quickly walked away;
Who was it, then, that came along and ministered that day? (Chorus)

From Jerusalem to Jericho a Levite came along,
Unheeding yet the cry of him who lay upon the ground,
He raised his hands up to the heavens and quickly walked away;
Who was it, then, that came along and ministered that day? (Chorus)

From Jerusalem to Jericho the wounded man did lay,
Along came that Samaritan, who was despised, they say;
He ministered unto the injured, took him to the inn,
He paid his fare and told the host to take good care of him. (Chorus)

From Jerusalem to Jericho we're traveling every day,
And many are the fallen ones that lie along the way,
They seem despised, rejected, but no matter what they've been,
When everybody casts them out, why, Jesus takes them in. (Chorus)

Give Me the Roses Now

James Rowe   Key of D   R.H. Cornelius

The Carter Family

James Rowe, who wrote the lyrics of "Give Me the Roses Now" was perhaps the most prolific gospel lyricist of all time. By his own guess, he wrote the lyrics to over 20,000 songs. If we take him at his word and then knock off 90% of them, that's still 2000 songs, no mean accomplishment! His other gospel classics include "If I Could Hear My Mother Pray Again" and "Love Lifted Me." An Englishman by birth, Rowe made his home in New York State but eventually moved to Lawrenceburg, Tennessee, to work with James D. Vaughan. Not to take anything away from James Rowe, but he wrote only lyrics, not melodies. For "Give Me the Roses Now" he collaborated in 1925 with R.H. Cornelius. It was first recorded in Camden, New Jersey, by The Carter Family on June 17, 1933. Artists who have recorded it include Jimmy Martin, Ralph Stanley and Wayne Erbsen. It is sometimes called "Give Me the Roses While I Live."

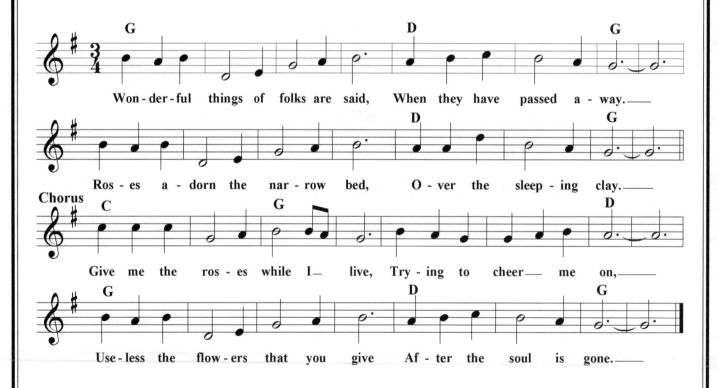

Won-der-ful things of folks are said, When they have passed a-way.—

Ros-es a-dorn the nar-row bed, O-ver the sleep-ing clay.—

Chorus

Give me the ros-es while I— live, Try-ing to cheer— me on,—

Use-less the flow-ers that you give Af-ter the soul is gone.—

Praises are heard not by the dead,
Roses they cannot see;
Let us not wait till souls have fled,
Generous friends to be. (Chorus)

Faults are forgiven when folks lie
Cold in the narrow bed;
Let us forgive them ere they die,
Now should the words be said. (Chorus)

The Glory-land Way

J.S. Torbett   Key of G   J.S. Torbett

Born in Gadsden, Alabama, in 1868, J.S. Torbett received his music training at A.J. Showalter's Southern Normal Music Institute. From there he taught singing schools for some thirty-five years. Torbett composed both the words and music to "The Glory-land Way," although the exact date is not known. It was first recorded by The McDonald Quartet on December 7, 1928. On January 27, 1938, J.E. Mainer & His Mountaineers recorded it in Charlotte, North Carolina, as a vocal duet with Leonard "Handsome" Stokes & George Morris.

I'm in the way, the bright and shin - ing way, I'm in the glo-ry-land way,——

Tell-ing the world that Je-sus saves to-day, Yes, I'm in the glo-ry-land way.——

I'm in the glo-ry-land way,——————   I'm in the glo-ry-land way,——

Heav-en is near-er and the way grow-eth clear-er, for I'm in the glo-ry-land way.——

List to the call, the gospel call today,
Get in the glory-land way,
Wanderers, come home, O hasten to obey,
For I'm in the glory-land way. (Chorus)

Onward I go, rejoicing in His love,
I'm in the glory-land way,
Soon I shall see Him in that home above,
Oh, I'm in the glory-land way. (Chorus)

The Good Old Way

Key of G

As   I went down in the val - ley to pray,

Stu-dy-ing a-bout that good old way. And who shall wear the

star - ry crown, Good   Lord, show me the way.

Chorus

Oh bro - thers, let's go down———— come on down, don't you

want to go down.———— Oh bro - thers. let's go down————

down in the val - ley to pray.

The Good Old Way

This old Black spiritual was first collected in 1867 in a book entitled *Slave Songs of the United States.* Although the lyrics were apparently from slave sources, the title may have been borrowed from "The Good Old Way," which was written and published in 1835 by the famed composer William Walker. "Singin' Billy" Walker (1809-1875), as he was known, was raised in Spartanburg, South Carolina, and was the compiler of a number of hymn books, including **Southern Harmony**. By the time of his death, Walker had sold more than 750,000 books.

Also known by its first line, "As I Went Down in the Valley to Pray," this song gained fame in the 2000 Coen brothers' film, "Oh Brother, Where Art Thou?" where the lyrics were changed to "As I went down to the river to pray." This was done, presumably, to adjust to the fact that the scene was filmed next to a river, not a valley.

When you're singing it, remember that the only variation is in the refrain, where the word "brother" changes to "sister" or "mother" the next time you sing it.

> As I went down in the valley to pray,
> Studying about that good old way,
> And who shall wear the starry crown,
> Good Lord, show me the way.
>
> Oh brothers, let's go down,
> Come on down, don't you want to go down,
> Oh brothers, let's go down,
> Down in the valley to pray.
>
> Oh fathers...
>
> Oh mothers...
>
> Oh sinners...

Rev. Robert Akers Tent Revival, Galax, Virginia

Photo by Terry Eiler

Grave on a Green Hillside

Aldine S. Kieffer   Key of G   Aldine S. Kieffer

There's a lit - tle grave on the green hill - side that lies to the morn - ing sun,

And our way - worn feet oft - en wan - der there When the cares of the day are done;

There we oft - en sit till the twi - light falls, And talk of the far - off land,

And we some - times feel in the twi - light there The soft
In the years to come we will calm - ly sleep In a

touch of the van - ished hand.
grave on the green hill - side.

Chorus

Grave on the green hill - side,   Grave on the green hill - side;

Grave on a Green Hillside

If Aldine S. Kieffer (1840-1904) did nothing else but compose "Grave on a Green Hillside" and "Twilight is Falling," he would have earned a place in the history of Southern gospel music. Fortunately, he did not stop there. An active composer, poet, singing-school teacher, and publisher, he has been called by *The Encyclopedia of American Gospel Music* "the single most important figure in the history of Southern gospel music." Kieffer composed "Grave on the Green Hillside" around 1872, and it was first recorded by The Carter Family in Camden, New Jersey, on February 14, 1929. The following lyrics were transcribed from *The Harvester,* a publication of The Ruebush-Kieffer Co of Dayton, Virginia. When the book was new it sold for 30 cents.

There's a little grave on the green hillside
That lies to the morning sun,
And our wayworn feet often wander there
When the cares of the day are done;
There we often sit till the twilight falls,
And talk of the far-off land,
And we sometimes feel in the twilight there
The soft touch of the vanished hand.

Grave on the green hillside,
Grave on the green hillside;
In the years to come we will calmly sleep
In a grave on the green hillside.

Ah! the land is full of the little graves,
In valley, and plain, and hill;
There's an angel, too, for each little grave,
And these angels some mission fill;
And I know not how, but I sometimes think
They lead us with gentle hand,
For a whisper falls on our willing ear
From the shores of a far-off land. (Chorus)

Photo by Gerri Johnson

Patton family cemetery

And these little graves are but wayside marks
That point to the far-off land,
And they speak to the soul of a better day,
Of a day that is near at hand;
Though we first must walk through the darksome vale,
Yet there Christ will be our Guide,
And we'll reach the shore of the far-off land
Through a grave on the green hillside. (Chorus)

The Hallelujah Side

Rev. Johnson Oatman, Jr.   Key of G   J. Howard Entwisle

Once a sin-ner far from Je-sus, I was per-ish-ing with cold, But the

bless-ed Sav-ior heard me when I cried; Then He threw His robe a-round me and He

led me to His fold, And I'm liv-ing on the hal-le-lu-jah side.
win-dows of my soul, And I'm liv-ing on the hal-le-lu-jah side.

Chorus

Oh, glo-ry be to Je-sus, let the hal-le-lu-jahs roll, Help me

ring the Sav-ior's prais-es far and wide, For I've op-ened up toward heav-en all the

Laurel Glen Regular Baptist Church, Allegheny County, NC

Photo by Terry Eiler

58

The Hallelujah Side

Only a handful of gospel composers have come close to enjoying the success of Rev. Johnson Oatman, Jr. Not only did he compose "The Hallelujah Side," but also "Hand in Hand With Jesus," "Higher Ground," "Count Your Blessings," and "No, Not One!" Born April 21, 1856, near Medford, New Jersey, Oatman studied to become an ordained minister but declined to have his own congregation, instead he concentrated on writing gospel songs while managing an insurance agency in Mt. Holly, New Jersey. "The Hallelujah Side" was published in 1898, with melody composed by J. Howard Entwisle, who also wrote the music to "Keep on the Sunny Side of Life."

The first to record "The Hallelujah Side" was Ernest V. Stoneman & His Dixie Mountaineers. On September 21, 1926, they recorded it for Victor. Since then, this classic gospel song has been recorded by The Tindley Quaker City Gospel Singers, Bill Gaither, The Chuck Wagon Gang, and The Country Gentlemen.

Frost Stoneman Family

Once a sinner far from Jesus, I was perishing with cold,
But the blessed Savior heard me when I cried,
Then He threw His robe around me and He led me to His fold,
And I'm living on the hallelujah side.

Oh, glory be to Jesus, let the hallelujahs roll,
Help me ring the Savior's praises far and wide,
For I've opened up toward heaven all the windows of my soul,
And I'm living on the hallelujah side.

Though the world may sweep around me with her dazzle and her dreams,
Yet I envy not her vanities and pride,
For my soul looks up to heaven, where the golden sunlight gleams,
And I'm living on the hallelujah side. (Chorus)

Not for all earth's golden million would I leave this precious place,
Though the tempter to persuade me oft has tried,
For I'm safe in God's pavilion, happy in His love and grace,
And I'm living on the hallelujah side. (Chorus)

Here the sun is always shining, here the sky is always bright,
'Tis no place for gloomy Christians to abide,
For my soul is filled with music and my heart with great delight,
And I'm living on the hallelujah side. (Chorus)

And upon the streets of glory, when we reach the other shore,
And have safely crossed the Jordan's rolling tide,
You will find me shouting "Glory" just outside my mansion door,
Where I'm living on the hallelujah side. (Chorus)

Hallelujah, We Shall Rise

J.E. Thomas   Key of G   J.E. Thomas

Born in Calhoun County, Arkansas, December 6, 1860, J.E. Thomas wrote this popular gospel song in 1904 and published it in *Kingdom Songs* #1 in 1916. It was recorded by The Carter Family, The Sauceman Brothers, and by The Stanley Brothers.

In the resurrection morning what a meeting it will be,
We shall rise (hallelujah!) We shall rise.
When our fathers and our mothers and our loved ones we shall see,
We shall rise (hallelujah!) We shall rise. (Chorus)

In the resurrection morning blessed thought it is so me,
We shall rise (hallelujah!) We shall rise.
I shall see my blessed Savior who so freely died for me,
We shall rise (hallelujah!) We shall rise. (Chorus)

Hand in Hand with Jesus

Rev. Johnson Oatman, Jr.   Key of E   L.D. Huffstutler

Two veteran gospel songwriters teamed up to produce this standard of Southern gospel music. Rev. Johnson Oatman was a prolific lyricist, having composed songs like "The Hallelujah Side," "Higher Ground," "Count Your Blessings" and "No, Not One!" The composer of the melody, Leonard D. Huffstutler, was born in Liberty, Alabama, on June 17, 1887, but grew up on a farm in Texas. As a boy Huffstutler learned to sing gospel songs from his mother. After attending Texas A & M College, Huffstutler studied music with J.B. Herbert, R.H. Cornelius, Homer Rodeheaver, and A.B. Sebren. He then went on to a lifelong career singing in quartets and teaching in singing schools for the Hartford Music Company and for the Stamps-Baxter Music Company. "Hand in Hand with Jesus" has appeared in at least thirty-nine long-out-of-print songbooks.

Once from my poor sin - sick soul, Christ did ev - 'ry bur - den roll,

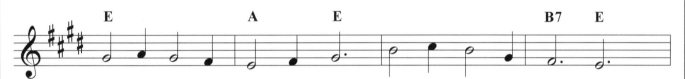

Now I walk re - deemed and whole, Hand in hand with Je - sus.

Chorus

Hand in hand we walk each day, Hand in hand a - long the way,

Walk - ing thus, I can - not stray, Hand in hand with Je - sus.

In my night of dark despair,
Jesus heard and answered prayer,
Now I'm walking free as air,
Hand in hand with Jesus. (Chorus)

From the straight and narrow way,
Praise the Lord, I cannot stray,
For I'm walking every day,
Hand in hand with Jesus. (Chorus)

He Will Set Your Fields on Fire

H.M. Ballew   Key of C   Mrs. L.L. Brackett

There's a call that rings for the one that sings, To those now gone a-stray, Say-ing

come ye men, and your load of sin, There at the al-ter lay; You don't

seem to heed, and the chain of greed, Your con-science ne-ver tires, Be as-

sured my friend, if you still of-fend, He will set your fields on fire.

Chorus If you don't re-tire set your

If you don't from sin re-tire, He will set your fields on

fields on fire, You have heard Je-sus call

soon your soul must fall Friend if

death you soon must fall, Now my friend if you de-

you de-sire join the heav'n-ly choir

sire, You may join the heav'n-ly choir, And re-

joice with Him-free from ev-'ry sin, He will set this world on fire.

He Will Set Your Fields on Fire

The bass-lead chorus of "He Will Set Your Fields on Fire" makes this one of the more challenging gospel songs to sing. The lyrics were written by H.M. Ballew and the melody was composed by Mrs. L.L. Brackett. Although we don't know the date it was composed, it appeared in a 1907 book entitled *Best of All, A Superior and Varied Collection of Gospel Songs and Hymns*, published in Dayton, Virginia.

First to record "He Will Set Your Fields on Fire" were Smith's Sacred Singers, who recorded it April 4, 1927. The Monroe Brothers recorded it in Charlotte, North Carolina, on August 3, 1937 in the same session that they recorded "On That Old Gospel Ship," "All the Good Times Are Passed And Gone," and "Sinner You Better Get Ready." Curiously, Bill Monroe, the tenor singer of the duo, sang bass on "He Will Set Your Fields on Fire." Even stranger is the fact that for this song he laid down his mandolin while brother Charlie

Monroe Brothers

accompanied them on his guitar. Could it be that this song was so challenging that Bill needed to concentrate on his bass singing?

There's a call that rings for the one that sings, to those now gone astray,
Saying come ye men, and your load of sin there at the alter {sic} lay;
You don't seem to heed, and the chain of greed your conscience never tires.
Be assured my friend, if you still offend, He will set your fields on fire. (Chorus)

  If you don't from sin retire, He will set your fields on fire;
  You have heard Jesus call, and in death you soon must fall.
  Now my friend, if you desire, you may join the heavenly choir,
  And rejoice with Him, free from every sin, when He sets this world on fire.

You have heard His voice, seen His soul rejoice, that trusted in His grace.
You have blushed with sin as He knocked within, but still you hide your face,
From the blessed Lord and His own true word, but still you say retire;
Leave the downward path, kindle not His wrath, or He'll set your fields on fire. (Chorus)

Won't you take advice, make the sacrifice, completely turn from sin.
Taking up the cross, counting pleasures dross, let Jesus live within;
When temptations come, you can face toward home, your heart will never tire.
But rejoice and pray in the last great day, when He sets this world on fire. (Chorus)

> *"I can put more in a sacred song that I can just an ordinary song. I can feel more, you know. I feel like I'm doing myself, and maybe other people too, more good."* Ralph Stanley

Heaven Above

Wayne Erbsen   ©1975 by Wayne Erbsen Fracas Music (BMI)   Wayne Erbsen

Chorus

Oh heaven a - bove, or hell be - low, heaven a - bove, Or hell be low, When you leave this world of sor row tell me where will you go, heaven a - bove, or hell be - low? You've been walk-in', you've been talk-in', Through this wick - ed world of sin, and you don't know where you're go - in' And you don't know where you've been.

You've been praying, you've been shouting,
And you think that you are saved.
But when the gates of hell are open,
Sinner, don't call out His name. (Chorus)

64

Heaven Above

While touring Germany in the winter of 1975, we stopped to look at the ruins of an ancient castle near the banks of the Rhine River. As we were passing through the last gate on our way out, I turned my head and looked upward to catch a last glimpse of the massive castle walls above me. As I did, my eyes looked skyward and I thought of the expression "heaven above." From that, I soon composed the song. Returning home after the European tour, I rejoined the Black Mountain Blue-grass Boys in West Virginia, playing fiddle and mandolin. During a quiet evening at home, I sang "Heaven Above" to the lead singer of the group, the late Harley Carpenter. I valued Harley's opinion because I knew that he

was not only one of bluegrass's best lead singers, but he also had very dyed-in-the-wool tastes when it came to music. I wanted to know whether my suspicions were correct in thinking that the verse of "Heaven Above" held the D chord for a little too long. After Harley took his guitar and sang the verse, he was adamant that I not change it.

Harley's opinion was reinforced several years later when I met Bill Monroe back stage at the Civic Center, when he played in my hometown of Asheville, North Carolina. I worked up my nerve and asked Bill if I could sing a song or two with him. He handed me his guitar player's D-28, and we sang several songs including Ernest Tubb's "Are You Waiting Just For Me." I knew I was on the right track when he told me that he hadn't sung that song since he sang it on the Opry with Lester Flatt back in the mid 'forties. This gave me the courage to take the bold step of asking Monroe if he would sing a song with me that I wrote, "Heaven Above." Bill encouraged me to try it. When it came time for the chorus, Bill sang after me, in call and response style. I had never thought of the song like that, and I realized that I was in effect "lining out" the song, just like in the old camp meeting days when hymn books were few and song leaders would sing or recite each line of a song for the other singers to follow. Bill said he really liked "Heaven Above," and promised to record it if I'd send him a tape of it. The next day I fired up my portable cassette recorder and sent the tape to Monroe's attention in Nashville, Tennessee. As you might have guessed, Bill never did record it, but I can still hear his spooky tenor as he sang the tenor part on the chorus of "Heaven Above."

Hold Fast to the Right

Anonymous　　　　　　　　　　　　Key of G　　　　　　　　　　James D. Vaughan

Hold Fast to the Right

Professional songsmiths of the late 19th and early 20th century catered to the public taste for ballads that were utterly dripping in sentimentality. Entire families often gathered in the parlor around the piano to sing songs of poor newsboys in tattered clothes, orphans standing barefoot in the snow, and wayward boys who left their dear, sick mothers to beg for bread. Today, some people laugh at these kinds of songs and refer to them as "tear jerkers," but back then, these sad laments were serious business. It wasn't until the Roaring Twenties, when popular culture produced the jazzy sounds of swing, that many Americans turned away from the songs that brought a tear to the eye and a heaviness of the heart. However, these types of sentimental songs remained popular in the rural South, the very audience that embraced Southern gospel music. The lyrics of "Hold Fast to the Right" sound like they came right out of the sentimental era of the 1890s when so many "mother" songs were popular. Although we can't trace the source of the lyrics, we know that James D. Vaughan composed the melody in 1906. First to record it were Lester McFarland & Robert A. Gardner on August 16, 1928. It was printed in *Mac and Bob's Book of Songs*, published by M.M. Cole Publishing Company, 1931.

Kneel down by the side of your mother, my boy,
You have only a moment I know,
But stay till I give you this parting advice,
It is all that I have to bestow.

Hold fast to the right, hold fast to the right,
Wherever your footsteps may roam,
Oh forsake not the way of salvation my boy,
That you learned from your mother at home.

You leave us to seek your employment, my boy,
By the world you have yet to be tried,
But in the temptations and trials you meet,
May your heart to the Savior confide. (Chorus)

I gave you to God in your cradle, my boy,
And I've taught you the best that I knew,
And as long as His mercies permit me to live,
I shall never cease praying for you. (Chorus)

You will find in your satchel a Bible, my boy,
It's the book of all others the best,
It will help you to live and prepare you to die,
And will lead to the gates of the blest. (Chorus)

Hold to God's Unchanging Hand

Jennie Wilson   Key of G   F.L. Eiland

Time   is   filled   with   swift   tran - si - tion,   Naught   of   earth   un - moved   can

stand,   Build   your   hopes   on   things   e - ter - nal,

Hold   to   God's   un - chang - ing   hand.   Hold   to

God's un - chang - ing   hand,   Hold   to   God's   un - chang - ing   hand,

Build your hopes on things e - ter - nal,   Hold   to   God's   un - chang - ing   hand.

Hold to God's Unchanging Hand

Few people start out with less and end up with more than the poet Jennie Wilson. Born on a farm near South Whitley, Indiana, in 1857, at the age of four she was struck with a spinal disease that left her an invalid. Unable to walk and bound to a wheel chair, Jenny could not attend school, so she received her education at home, which included some music training. Her creative spirit took her where her legs could not, and she was said to have written over 2,200 poems in her fifty-six years. "Hold to God's Unchanging Hand" was published in 1905

Roy Acuff

and has been reprinted in at least thirty-four songbooks. First to record it was The Vaughan Quartet on November 3, 1926. Later groups who recorded "Hold to God's Unchanging Hand" include Smith's Sacred Singers, Roy Acuff, The Stanley Brothers, Jimmy Martin, Bill Gaither, Porter Wagner, and Rev. Gary Davis.

Time is filled with swift transition,
Naught of earth unmoved can stand,
Build your hopes on things eternal,
Hold to God's unchanging hand.

   Hold (to His hand) to God's unchanging hand,
   Hold (to His hand) to God's unchanging hand,
   Build your hopes on things eternal,
   Hold to God's unchanging hand.

Trust in Him who will not leave you,
Whatsoever years may bring,
If by earthly friends forsaken,
Still more closely to Him cling. (Chorus)

Covet not this world's vain riches,
That so rapidly decay,
Seek to gain the heavenly treasures,
They will never pass away. (Chorus)

When your journey is completed,
If to God you have been true,
Fair and bright the home in glory,
Your enraptured soul may view. (Chorus)

> *"Do not fan violently in church."* Social Conduct, 1934

Home in That Rock

Key of D

This old spiritual became a bluegrass song when Flatt & Scruggs recorded it as "God Gave Noah the Rainbow Sign," which they learned from The Carter Family. This version has a minor flavor and was collected in Georgia in the 1920s by Dorothy G. Bolton in *Old Songs Hymnal*, published in 1929.

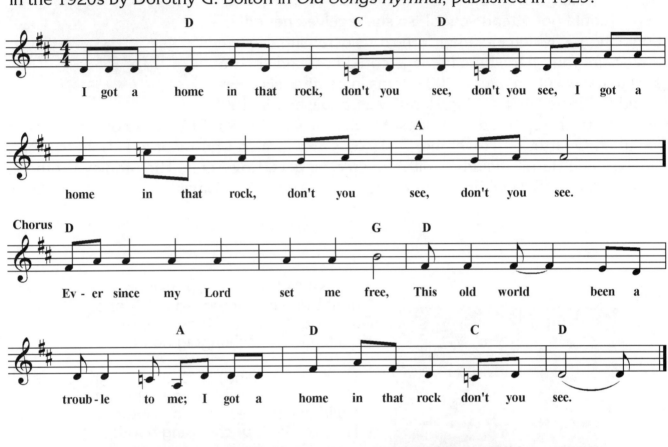

I got a home in that rock, don't you see, don't you see, I got a home in that rock, don't you see, don't you see.

Chorus

Ev-er since my Lord set me free, This old world been a trou-ble to me; I got a home in that rock don't you see.

Photo by Roy Stryker

Gospel Mission, Minneapolis, Minnesota, 1937

Home in That Rock

Photo by Lyntha Eiler

Laurel Glen Regular Baptist Church, Allegheny County, NC

I got a home in that rock,
Don't you see, don't you see,
I got a home in that rock,
Don't you see, don't you see.

Ever since my Lord set me free,
This old world been a trouble to me,
I got a home in that rock,
Don't you see.

I got a home where the gambler can't come,
Don't you see, don't you see,
I got a home where the gambler can't come,
Don't you see, don't you see. (Chorus)

I got a home where liars can't come,
Don't you see, don't you see,
I got a home where liars can't come,
Don't you see, don't you see. (Chorus)

I got a home where drunkards can't come,
Don't you see, don't you see,
I got a home where drunkards can't come,
Don't you see, don't you see, (Chorus)

When I get to heaven I'll shout and tell,
Don't you see, don't you see,
When I get to heaven I'll shout and tell,
Don't you see, don't you see. (Chorus)

How Beautiful Heaven Must Be

Mrs. A.S. Bridgewater   Key of G   A.P. Bland

We read of a place that's called hea - ven, It's made for the pure and the free,— These truths in God's Word He hath giv - en, How beau - ti - ful heav - en must be.—

Chorus
How beau - ti - ful heav - en must be,— Sweet home of the hap - py and free,— Fair ha - ven of rest for the wear - y, How beau - ti - ful - heav - en must be.—

"If you treat people right you don't have to be in church every Sunday, and if you don't, there ain't no use a-goin.' Edd Michels

How Beautiful Heaven Must Be

Y ou only have to look at the list of artists who have recorded "How Beautiful Must Be" to appreciate its widespread popularity and appeal: Eva Quartet, Riley Quartet, North Georgia Quartet, The Vagabonds, Asher Sizemore & Little Jimmie, W. Lee O'Daniel & His Light Crust Doughboys, Knippers Brothers & Parker, Newman Brothers, Dick Hartman's Tennessee Rambers, The Prairie Ramblers, The Monroe Brothers, Uncle Dave Macon, Roy Acuff, George Jones, Rose Maddox, The Stanley Brothers, Porter Wagoner, The Marksmen and Carl Story. Notice that these artists represent many diverse styles, including old-time gospel, bluegrass gospel, old-time country, traditional country, western swing and stringband music.

> "Every show had to have a gospel song, such as ...
> 'How Beautiful Heaven Must Be.'" Pee Wee King

We read of a place that's called heaven,
It's made for the pure and the free,
These truths in God's Word He hath given,
How beautiful heaven must be.

　How beautiful heaven must be (must be),
　Sweet home of the happy and free,
　Fair haven of rest for the weary,
　How beautiful heaven must be.

In heaven no drooping nor pining,
No wishing for elsewhere to be,
God's light is forever there shining,
How beautiful heaven must be. (Chorus)

Pure waters of life there are flowing,
And all who will drink may be free,
Rare jewels of splendor are glowing,
How beautiful heaven must be. (Chorus)

The angels so sweetly are singing,
Up there by the beautiful sea,
Sweet chords from their gold harps are ringing,
How beautiful heaven must be. (Chorus)

Photo by Pat Mullen

Floyd County, Virginia

I Am a Pilgrim

Key of G

Although closely associated with Merle Travis, "I Am a Pilgrim" has roots than run much deeper than his 1946 recording for King Records. In fact, Travis apparently learned it from Mose Rager. As folklorist Kip Lornell has pointed out in the notes to "Classic Southern Gospel from Smithsonian Folkways," it was recorded by fourteen African-American groups before it was even a gleam in Merle Travis' eyes. The song was a favorite of Carl Story, who is often called the "Father of Bluegrass Gospel Music." As a boy, Carl Story's father used to take him to the courthouse in Lenoir, North Carolina, to hear his idol,

Merle Travis

Riley Puckett. It was from Puckett that Story learned "I Am a Pilgrim." Over the years the song has been recorded by such artists as Chet Atkins, The Byrds, Johnny Cash, Charlie Daniels, David Grisman, The Country Gentlemen, Grandpa Jones, The Kentucky Colonels, The Nitty Gritty Dirt Band, and Bill Monroe.

I'm going down to the river of Jordan,
Just to ease my troubled soul;
If I could touch but the hem of His garment, good Lord,
I do believe it would make me whole. (Chorus)

I've got a mother, a sister and a brother,
Who have gone on before;
And I'm determined to go and meet them, good Lord,
Over on that other shore. (Chorus)

I Am Bound For the Promised Land

Samuel Stennett   Key of D

Also known as "On Jordan's Story Bank I Stand," the lyrics of "I Am Bound For the Promised Land" were written by Samuel Stennett in 1787 and apparently arranged in 1840 by Miss M. Durham. It is commonly found in shaped-note hymn books.

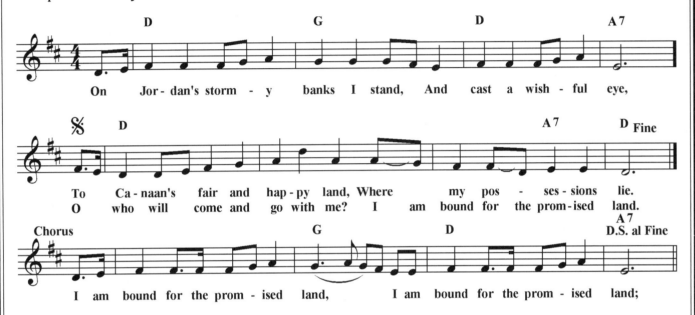

On Jor-dan's storm - y banks I stand, And cast a wish - ful eye,

To Ca - naan's fair and hap - py land, Where my pos - ses - sions lie.
O who will come and go with me? I am bound for the prom-ised land.

Chorus

I am bound for the prom - ised land, I am bound for the prom - ised land;

All o'er those wide extended plains shines one eternal day;
There God the Son forever reigns, and scatters night away. (Chorus)

No chilling winds, nor poisonous breath, can reach that healthful shore;
Sickness and sorrow, pain and death, are felt and feared no more. (Chorus)

When shall I reach that happy place, and be forever blest?
When shall I see my Father's face, and in His bosom rest? (Chorus)

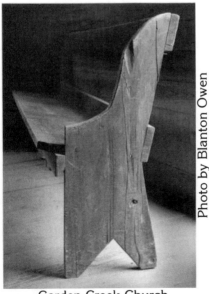

Garden Creek Church

Photo by Blanton Owen

I Feel Like Traveling On

ca. 1912

William Hunter, D.D. Key of G William Hunter, D.D.

My heav'n-ly home is bright and fair, I feel like trav-el-ing on, No pain, nor death can en-ter there, I feel like trav-el-ing on.

Chorus

trav-el-ing on,
Yes, I feel like trav-el-ing on, I

trav-el-ing on,
feel like trav-el-ing on, My heav'n-ly home is

bright and fair, I feel like trav-el-ing on.

Its glittering towers the sun outshine,
I feel like traveling on,
That heavenly mansion shall be mine,
I feel like traveling on. (Chorus)

Let others seek a home below,
I feel like traveling on,
Which flames devour, or waves o'er-flow,
I feel like traveling on. (Chorus)

Be mine a happier lot to own,
I feel like traveling on,
A heavenly mansion near the throne,
I feel like traveling on. (Chorus)

The Lord has been so good to me,
I feel like traveling on,
Until that blessed home I see
I feel like traveling on. (Chorus)

I Have Found the Way

Rev. L.E. Green Key of G Adger M. Pace

This classic of old-time Southern gospel was composed by Rev. L.E. Green and Adger M. Pace. Pace was originally from Pelzer, South Carolina, but grew up on a farm in Georgia. Showing an early interest in music at fifteen-years-old, he directed his church choir, and at seventeen, he wrote his first song. A lifelong singer, composer, and singing-school teacher, he was editor for Vaughan Publishing Company and first president of the National Singing Convention. His most popular composition is "Beautiful Star of Bethlehem."

I will never fear while Jesus is so near,
I will bravely meet the foe,
Happy songs I'll sing in honor to the King,
And to glory onward go. (Chorus)

To the journey's end led by a faithful Friend,
Nevermore in sin to roam,
By the way called straight I'll reach the golden gate,
Of the soul's eternal home. (Chorus)

I Heard My Mother Call My Name in Prayer

E.M. Bartlett   Key of G   E.M. Bartlett

While kneel-ing by her bed-side, on the cot-tage on the hill, My

moth-er prayed her blessings on me there; She was talk-ing then to Je-sus while
and He

ev - 'ry-thing was still, and I heard my moth-er call my name in prayer.
saved my soul from sin. For He heard my moth-er call my name in prayer.

Chorus

Yes, I heard my moth-er call my name in prayer, She was

pour-ing out her heart to Je-sus there, then I gave my heart to Him

Photo by Lyntha Eller

Bessie Brooks

78

I Heard My Mother Call My Name in Prayer

Bluegrass and country musicians have always had a soft spot for songs about mother. Little wonder this song has long been popular with artists like Red Allen, Mac Wiseman, Ricky Skaggs, and The Nashville Grass. "I Heard My Mother Call My Name in Prayer" was written in 1919 by Eugene Monroe Bartlett, a pioneer of Southern gospel music. Born on December 24, 1884 in Waynesville, Missouri, Bartlett took his passion for music and helped form Hartford Music Company in 1918. In addition to producing numerous gospel songbooks, Bartlett taught singing-schools, sponsored touring quartets, and published a monthly magazine, *The Herald of Song*. Bartlett authored a number of songs that have become classics of Southern gospel, including "Victory in Jesus," "Everybody Will Be Happy Over There," and "Just a Little While to Stay Here." He is also the unlikely composer of "Take an Old Cold Tater And Wait," a career song for Little Jimmy Dickens. Perhaps Bartlett's biggest contribution was mentoring a young man named Albert E. Brumley. In early 1926 this twenty-one-year-old showed up at Bartlett's door with $2.50 in his pocket, wanting to learn to compose gospel songs. Brumley went on to compose such all-time classics as "I'll Fly Away," "Turn Your Radio On," "Rank Strangers," "If We Never Meet Again," "I'll Meet You in the Morning," and literally hundreds of some of the best loved songs in gospel music.

While kneeling by her bedside on the cottage on the hill,
My mother prayed her blessings on me there;
She was talking then to Jesus while everything was still,
And I heard my mother call my name in prayer.

   Yes, I heard my mother call my name in prayer,
   She was pouring out her heart to Jesus there,
   Then I gave my heart to Him and He saved my soul from sin,
   For He heard my mother call my name in prayer.

She was anxious for her boy to be just what he ought to be,
And she asked the Lord to take him in His care;
Just the words I can't remember but I know she prayed for me,
For I heard my mother call my name in prayer. (Chorus)

How my heart was touched and tendered by the prayer that mother prayed!
I can almost see her form now kneeling there,
As she told her Lord and Savior just how far from Him I strayed,
Yes I heard my mother call my name in prayer. (Chorus)

Then I gave my heart to Jesus and am living now for Him,
And some day I'll go to meet Him in the air;
For He heard my mother praying and has saved my soul from sin,
Yes He heard my mother call my name in prayer. (Chorus)

I Will Never Turn Back

R. N. Graham   Key of G   R.N. Graham

Once I wan - dered in dark - ness un - saved, Till the
Sav - ior came knock - ing at my heart, And I o - pened the door, let Him
in, Now rich bless - ings to me He im - parts.

Chorus
ne - ver turn back, ne - ver turn back,
I will ne - - - er turn back, He's my
He is my light ev - 'ry hour and day, ne - ver turn back,
light ev - 'ry day; No, I'll ne - - - ver turn
ne - ver turn back.
back, For my Sav - ior is lead - ing the way.

Of His love I will sing every day,
Yes, I'll sing of His wondrous power to save,
For my Savior is leading the way,
To those mansions of glory above. (Chorus)

In His service each day may I be,
Leading sinners to Jesus to be healed,
Through the blood flowing from Calvary,
Till the light of His love they behold. (Chorus)

80

I Would Not Be Denied

Charles P. Jones   Key of D   Charles P. Jones

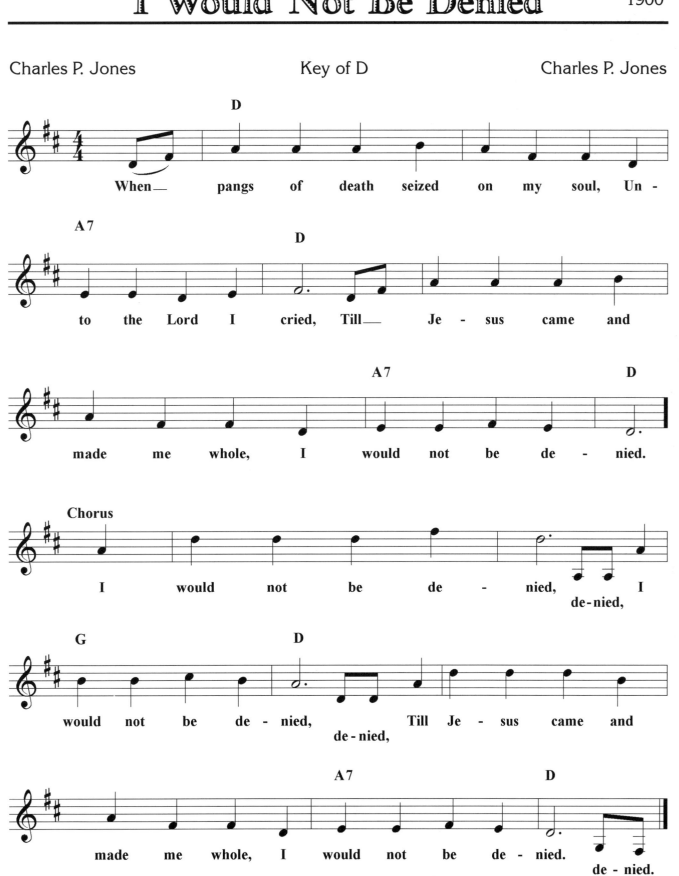

When — pangs of death seized on my soul, Unto the Lord I cried, Till — Je - sus came and
made me whole, I would not be de - nied.

Chorus

I would not be de - nied, I de-nied, I
would not be de - nied, de-nied, Till Je - sus came and
made me whole, I would not be de - nied. de-nied.

As Jacob in the days of old,
I wrestled with the Lord,
And instant with a courage bold,
I stood upon His word. (Chorus)

Old Satan said my Lord was gone
And would not hear my prayer,
But praise the Lord! the work is done,
And Christ, the Lord is here. (Chorus)

If I Could Hear My Mother Pray Again

James Rowe   Key of G   J.W. Vaughan

How sweet and hap-py seem those days of which I dream, When mem-o-ry re-calls them now and then! And with what rap-ture sweet my wea-ry heart would beat, If I could hear my moth-er pray a-gain.
so much to me, If I could hear my moth-er pray a-gain.

Chorus
If I could hear my moth-er pray a-gain, If
If I could on-ly
I could hear her ten-der voice as then! So glad I'd be, 'twould mean
I could on-ly hap-py I should

If I Could Hear My Mother Pray Again

Songs about mother have always had a strange allure to bluegrass musicians. In terms of popularity, "If I Could Hear My Mother Pray Again" is certainly the "mother" of all mother songs. It was first recorded on April 21, 1926 by Jake Pickell, who sang it and played the ukulele. Country and bluegrass musicians who recorded it include the Callahan Family, Wade Mainer & Zeke Morris, Roy Acuff, The Blue Sky Boys, Hylo Brown, Jimmie Davis, Loretta Lynn, George Jones, Charlie Louvin, Carl Story and Mac Wiseman.

The lyrics of "If I Could Hear My Mother Pray Again" were written in 1922 by James Rowe (1865-1933), who is widely regarded as the most prolific nineteenth century gospel lyricist. Born in England, Rowe spent most of his life in New York state. His claim to have written over 20,000 songs has never been chal-

Wade Mainer

lenged. Although Rowe was a master lyricist, he apparently never wrote a single note of melody. For "If I Could Hear My Mother Pray Again," he turned to an Alabama native named John Whitefield Vaughan to compose the melody. Vaughan, who has often been referred to as J.W. Vaughan, is often confused with J.D. Vaughan, with whom he studied music.

Photo by Lyntha Eller

Crossroads Primitive Baptist Church, Baywood, Virginia

How sweet and happy seem those days of which I dream,
When memory recalls them now and then,
And with what rapture sweet my weary heart would beat,
If I could hear my mother pray again.

If I could (only) hear, my mother pray again,
If I could (only) hear her tender voice as then!
So glad (happy I should) I'd be,
'Twould mean so much to me,
If I could hear my mother pray again.

She used to pray that I on Jesus would rely,
And always walk the shining gospel way;
So trusting still His love, I seek that home above,
Where I shall meet my mother some glad day. (Chorus)

Within the old home-place, her patient, smiling face,
Was always spreading comfort, hope and cheer;
And when she used to sing to her eternal King,
It was the songs the angels loved to hear. (Chorus)

Her work on earth is done, the life-crown has been won,
And she will be at rest with Him above;
And some glad morning she, I know will welcome me,
To that eternal home of peace and love. (Chorus)

I'll Be No Stranger There

J.H. Alcon   Key of G   A.B. Sebren

A.B. Sebren, who wrote the melody of "I'll Be No Stranger There," was only eleven years old when he attended his first singing-school. Born in Belmont, Louisiana, on August 25, 1879, he eventually went on to study with F.F. Eiland ("Hold to God's Unchanging Hand,") and Emmett S. Dean ("Just Over in the Gloryland"). Sebren went on to become one of the greatest gospel singers and teachers of his time. He sang and managed quartets for The Trio Music Company, The Quartet Music Company, The James D. Vaughan Company, and The Sebren Music Company. The verses to "I'll Be No Stranger There" are a great place to use the technique of call and response.

I'll Be No Stranger There

I'm in the way (I'm in the way), the narrow way (the narrow way),
To mansions bright (to mansions bright) and fair (so bright and fair).
With friends I'll be (with friends I'll be) so glad and free (so glad and free),
I'll be no stran-(I'll be no stranger) ger there (no stranger there).

   I'll be no stranger there, I'll be no stranger there,
   When all the saved come from the grave, I'll be no stranger there.
   I'll be no stranger there, I'll be no stranger there,
   When all the saved come from the grave, I'll be no stranger there.

The Lord will call (the Lord will call), both great and small (both great and small),
To mansions bright (to mansions bright) and fair (so bright and fair).
To heaven above (to heaven above) where all is love (where all is love),
I'll be no stran- (I'll be no stranger) ger there (no stranger there). (Chorus)

My path is bright (my path is bright), my burdens light (my burdens light),
I have a home (I have a home) up there (a home up there).
I'll sing His praise (I'll sing His praise) through countless days (through countless days)
I'll be no stran- (I'll be no stranger) ger there (no stranger there). (Chorus)

My Savior stands (my Savior stands) with outstretched hands (with outstretched hands),
He's calling me (he's calling me) up there (calling up there).
His voice I hear (His voice I hear), I have no fear (I have no fear).
I'll be no stran- (I'll be no stranger) ger there (no stranger there). (Chorus)

Photo by Jack Delano

The Lemuel Smith family, Carrol County, Virginia, 1941

85

I'm Going That Way

James Rowe   Key of A   L.B. Register

I've heard of a land of joy and peace and won-der-ful light, and won-der-ful light,

A beau-ti-ful place of man-sions fair and skies ev-er bright, and skies ev-er bright,

Where all who be-lieve the Sav-ior dear, for-ev-er shall stay, for-ev-er shall stay,

And hav-ing been saved by grace di-vine, I'm go-ing that way.

Chorus

I'm go-ing that way, I'm on that way I'm go-ing that way, I'm go-ing that way.

1

And Je-sus that Sav-ior I a-dore is with me each day, is with me each day,

2

Yes, sing-ing His prais-es all day long, I'm go-ing that way. I'm go-ing that way.

I'm Going That Way

I've heard of a land of joy and peace and wonderful light, (and wonderful light),
A beautiful place of mansions fair and skies ever bright, (and skies ever bright);
Where all who believe the Savior dear, forever shall stay, (forever shall stay),
And having been saved by grace divine, I'm going that way. (Chorus)

    I'm going that way, (I'm on my way), I'm going that way, (I'm going that way),
    And Jesus the Savior I adore is with me each day; (is with me each day);
    I'm clinging to Him, (I cling to Him), and never to stray, (and never to stray),
    Yes, singing His praises all day long, I'm going that way, (I'm going that way).

The glorious news I tell and sing, as onward I go (as onward I go),
That those who are still astray in sin my Savior may know (my Savior shall know),
I want them to sing His praises above, some beautiful day (some beautiful day)
For glory to Him who died for me, I'm going that way. (Chorus)

I know I shall meet Him at the gate, when trials are past (when trials are past),
I know I shall meet Him face to face in glory at last (in glory at last),
And oh, I believe that when we meet "well done" He will say ("well done" he will say),
For trusting His soul to redeeming love, I'm going that way. (Chorus)

Photo by Terry Eiler

Laurel Glen Regular Baptist Church, Allegheny County, NC

I'm Going Through

Herbert Buffum   Key of G   Herbert Buffum

I'm Going Through

Composed in 1908 by Herbert Buffum, "I'm Going Through" was recorded by The Monroe Brothers in Charlotte, North Carolina, June 21, 1936. Originally written in waltz time as "I'm Going Through, Jesus," The Monroe Brothers changed the rhythm from 3/4 to a fast 4/4 time.

Lord I have started to walk in the light,
Shining upon me from heaven so bright;
I bade the world and its follies adieu,
I've started in Jesus, and I'm going through.

I'm going through, yes, I'm going through;
I'll pay the price, whatever others do;
I'll take the way with the Lord's despised few,
I'm going through, Jesus, I'm going through.

Many they are who start in the race;
But with the light they're fuse [sic] to keep pace;
Others accept it because it is new,
But not very many expect to go through. (Chorus)

I'd rather walk with Jesus alone,
And have for a pillow, like Jacob, a stone,
Living each moment with His face in view,
Than shrink from my pathway and fail to go through. (Chorus)

O brother, now will you take up the cross?
Give up the world, and count it as dross;
Sell all thou hast, and give to the poor,
Then go through with Jesus and those who endure. (Chorus)

Photo by Marion Post Wolcott

Campton, Kentucky, September 1940

I'm S-A-V-E-D

ecorded first by Gid Tanner & Fate Norris on April 20, 1926, this novelty song has brought forth more than its share of chuckles over the years. The Georgia Yellow Hammers recorded "I'm S-A-V-E-D" August 9, 1927, with an additional verse which was borrowed from a Harry Bennett novelty song from about 1877 called "The Bald Headed End of a Broom."

When married folks have a lot of cash their love is firm and strong
But when they have to live on hash their love don't last so long,
With a cross-eyed baby on each knee and a wife with a plaster on her nose,
I tell you, boys, it's no great fun when you have to wear second-hand clothes.

The best known version of "I'm S-A-V-E-D" was recorded by The Blue Sky Boys February 5, 1940 at the Kimball House, 30 South Tryon Street (rooms 104 & 106), Atlanta, Georgia. Bill Bollick remembers first hearing it at a singing convention or camp meeting in Hickory, North Carolina, sponsored by the First Church of God.

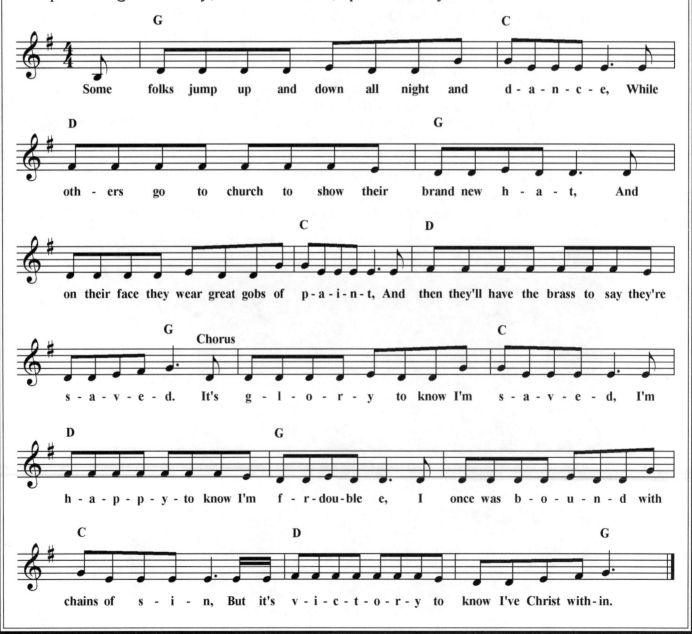

I'm S-A-V-E-D

Key of G

Some folks jump up and down all night and d-a-n-c-e,
While others go to church to show their brand new h-a-t,
And on their face they put great gobs of p-a-i-n-t,
And then they'll have the brass to say they're s-a-v-e-d.

   It's g-l-o-r-y to know I'm s-a-v-e-d,
   I'm h-a-p-p-y to know I'm f-r double-e,
   I once was b-o-u-n-d with the chains of s-i-n,
   But it's v-i-c-t-o-r-y to know I've Christ within.

I've seen some girls in our town who are n-i-c-e,
They do their hair in the latest style, just b-o-b-e-d,
They go to parties every night, drink w-i-n-e,
And then they have the nerve to say they're s-a-v-e-d. (Chorus)

I've seen some boys lean back and puff their s-m-o-k-e,
While others chew and spit out all their j-u-i-c-e,
They play their cards and shoot their guns and drink their p-o-p,
And then they'll have the brass to say they're s-a-v-e-d. (Chorus)

I know a man, I think his name's B-r-o-w-n,
He prays for Prohibition and he votes for g-i-n,
He helps put the poison in his neighbor's c-u-p,
And then he'll have the brass to say he's s-a-v-e-d. (Chorus)

In the Garden

C. Austin Miles   Key of G   C. Austin Miles

I come to the gar - den a - lone, While the

dew is still on the ro - ses; And the voice I hear, Fall - ing

on my ear; The Son of God dis - clos - es.

Chorus
And He walks with me, and He talks with me, and He

tells me I am His own, And the joy we share as we

tar - ry there, None oth-er has ev - er known.

In the Garden

A pharmacist by profession, C. Austin Miles' real passion was writing religious songs. His first song, "List 'Tis Jesus' Voice" was written in 1892 and published by the Hall-Mack Company. The song so impressed the company's owner, Dr. Adam Geibel, that Miles was hired as an editor. In 1912, Miles composed "In the Garden" after reading the twentieth chapter of John which told of Mary, Peter, and John visiting the tomb. It is widely regarded as among the most popular hymns of the twentieth century. It has been recorded by at least four hundred different artists.

I come to the garden alone,
While the dew is still on the roses,
And the voice I hear, falling on my ear;
The Son of God discloses.

And He walks with me, and He talks with me,
And He tells me I am His own,
And the joy we share as we tarry there,
None other has ever known.

He speaks, and the sound of His voice,
Is so sweet the birds hush their singing,
And the melody that He gave to me,
Within my heart is ringing. (Chorus)

I'd stay in the garden with Him,
Though the night around me be falling,
But He bids me go; Through the voice of woe,
His voice to me is calling. (Chorus)

Photo by Carl Fleischhaer

Mountain View Baptist Church   Low Gap, North Carolina
Built Around 1890

"It is as a writer of gospel songs I am proud to be known, for in that way I may be of the most use to my Master, whom I serve willingly although not as efficiently as is my desire." C. Austin Miles

In the Sweet By and By

Sanford Fillmore Bennett   Key of G   Joseph. P. Webster

The lyrics of this popular hymn were written in 1868 by Sanford Bennett, whose career included working as a druggist, superintendent of schools in Richmond, Illinois, editor of a weekly newspaper and second lieutenant in the Fortieth Wisconsin Volunteers during the Civil War. Joseph P. Webster, the composer of the lyrics of "In the Sweet By and By," is best known as the composer of the classic Civil War song, "Lorena." Evidence also points to Webster as the composer of the music to the popular bluegrass song, "The Wildwood Flower."

There's a land that is fair - er than day, And by faith we can see it a-
far; For the Fath-er waits o - ver the way, To pre - pare us a dwel-ling place there.

Chorus
In the sweet (In the sweet) by - and - by, (by - and - by) We shall
meet on that beau - ti - ful shore; (by - and - by;) In the sweet (In the sweet) by - and-
by, (by - and - by,) We shall meet on that beau - ti - ful shore.

We shall sing on that beautiful shore,
The melodious songs of the blest,
And our spirits shall sorrow no more,
Not a sigh for the blessing of rest. (Chorus)

To our bountiful Father above,
We will offer our tribute of praise,
For the glorious gift of His love,
And the blessings that hallow our days. (Chorus)

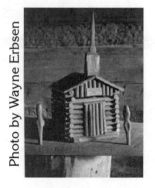

Photo by Wayne Erbsen

I've Just Seen the Rock of Ages

Key of A

Words & Music by John B. Preston, Markyle Music (BMI).

Photo by Glen Rose

Larry Sparks

Here is one of the true classics of bluegrass gospel music. Not much is known about the John B. Presion, the composer of the words and music of "I've Just seen the Rock of Ages." What is known is that he was apparently from Kentucky and spent some time in prison. His other compositions include "Running Bear," "Snap a Finger, Jesus," and "Walking Up This Hill on Decoration Day." Both Ralph Stanley and Larry Sparks have made "I've Just Seen the Rock of Ages" their signature song. Thanks to Mark and David Freeman of Rebel Records for their kind permission to print the words and music to this heartfelt song.

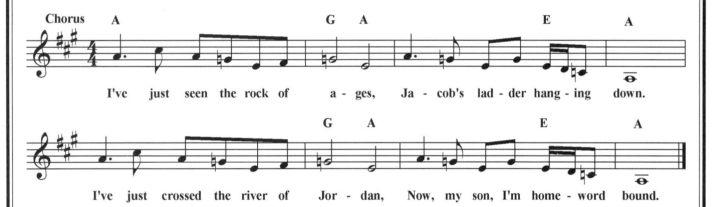

I've just seen the rock of a - ges, Ja - cob's lad - der hang - ing down.

I've just crossed the river of Jor - dan, Now, my son, I'm home - word bound.

I was standing by the bedside,
Where my feeble mother lay.
When she called me close beside her
And I thought I heard her say. (Chorus)

As we gathered all around her,
The tears begin to fill our eyes.
Then she called me close beside her
Whispered softly her good-bye. (Chorus)

High breeze blowing 'cross the mountain,
Where forever she will lay.
There she'll rest beside the fountain,
There she'll sleep beneath the clay. (Chorus)

Jesus, Savior, Pilot Me

Edward Hopper   Key of G   John E. Gould

This classic sacred gospel song was first published anonymously as a poem in *The Sailor's Magazine* in 1871. John E. Gould, who owned a music store in New York City, noticed the poem and set it to music but was never able to find out who wrote the poem. Gould published the hymn in 1871 in *The Baptist Praise Book*. In 1880 the true identity of the poem's composer was revealed to be the Reverend Edward Hopper, who was minister of the Church of Sea and Land in New York harbor. It was first recorded by The Friendship Quartet on February 23, 1928 in Memphis, Tennessee. It has since been recorded by Flatt & Scruggs, The Stanley Brothers, The McKameys, and George Morgan.

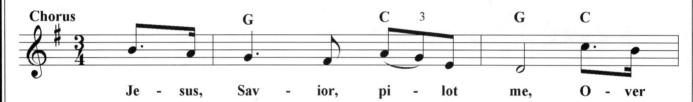

Je - sus, Sav - ior, pi - lot me, O - ver

life's tem - pest - uous sea, Un - known waves be - fore me

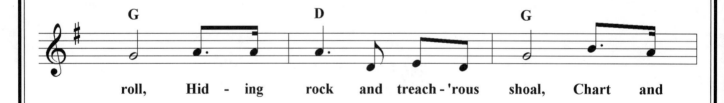

roll, Hid - ing rock and treach - 'rous shoal, Chart and

com - pass came— from - Thee, Je - sus, Sav - ior, pi - lot me.

As a mother stills her child,
Thou canst hush the ocean wild,
Boisterous waves obey Thy will,
When Thou sayest to them "Be still,"
Wondrous Sovereign of the sea,
Jesus, Savior, pilot me. (Chorus)

When at last I near the shore,
And the fearful breakers roar,
'Twixt me and peaceful rest,
Then, while leaning on Thy breast,
May I hear Thee say to me,
"Fear not, I will pilot thee." (Chorus)

Just a Closer Walk with Thee

Key of A

Although difficult to trace, most writers agree that "Just a Closer Walk with Thee" originated as a Black spiritual sometime before the Civil War. The identity of the composer remains a mystery. In his book *How Sweet the Sound*, Horace Clarence Boyer relates a story of how the song was "discovered." While traveling by train between Kansas City and Chicago in 1940, songwriter Kenneth Morris got off the train to stretch his legs. While standing on the platform, he overheard a porter singing some of the words to "Just a Closer Walk with Thee." Not thinking much about it, Morris boarded the train and went on his way. The words and melody of the song kept repeating in his head and he knew he had to learn the rest of it. At the next stop, Morris got off the train and took the next train back to the previous stop. There he managed to find the porter and Morris persuaded him to sing the song while he copied down the words. Morris soon added to the lyrics and published it in 1940. In the following years, the song has been translated into eleven languages and has appeared on over 600 albums as recorded by such diverse artists as Red Foley, Elvis Presley, Patsy Cline, Judy Collins, Jimmy Dean, Charlie Daniels, Ella Fitzgerald, Tennessee Ernie Ford, Roy Acuff, The Chuck Wagon Gang, Pete Fountain, Bob Dylan, Jesse Fuller, Merle Haggard, Mahalia Jackson, The Jordanaires, Little Richard, Loretta Lynn, Bob Margolin, and The Oak Ridge Boys. "Just a Closer Walk with Thee" is normally sung as a solo.

I am weak, but Thou art strong, Je - sus, keep me from all
Chorus: Just a clo - ser walk with Thee, Grant it Je - sus is my

wrong,_____ I'll be sat - is - fied as long,_____ As I
plea,_____ Dai - ly walk-ing close to Thee,_____ Let it

walk, let me walk close to Thee.
be,_____ Oh Lord, let it be.

Through this world of toil and snares,   When my feeble life is o'er,
If I falter, Lord, who cares?   Time for me will be no more,
Who with me my burden shares?   Guide me gently, safely o'er,
None but Thee, dear Lord, none but Thee.   To Thy kingdom shore, to Thy shore.

> "'Just A Closer Walk with Thee' put us on the map." Kenneth Morris

Just One Way to the Gate

There are man-y paths _____ thro' this world of sin, _____
There are man-y paths thro' this world of sin,

But there's on-ly one _____ I shall trav-el in; _____
But there's on-ly one I shall trav - el in

'Tis the old Cross Road, _____ or the way called "Straight" _____
'Tis the old Cross Road, or the way called "Straight"

there is just one way _____ to the pear-ly gate. _____
There is just one way to the pear - ly gate.

Chorus
There is just one way _____ to the pear-ly gate, _____ To the crown of
there is just one way to the pear-ly gate

life _____ and the friends who wait _____ 'Tis the old Cross
to the crown of life and the friends who wait

Road, _____ or the way called "Straight" _____ There is just one
'Tis the old Cross Road or the way called "Straight"

way _____ to the pear - ly gate _____
There is just one way to the pear-ly gate.

98

Just One Way to the Gate

James Rowe   Key of D   James D. Vaughan

Photo by Doris Ulmann, 1930

Written in 1920 with lyrics by James Rowe and melody by James D. Vaughan, the first one to record "Just One Way to the Gate" was Uncle Dave Macon, who waxed it in Richmond, Indiana, with Sam & Kirk McGee on August 14, 1934. However, this recording was never issued. Macon recorded it a second time for Bluebird on January 22, 1935. Wade Mainer, Zeke Morris, and Homer Sherrill recorded their version in Charlotte, North Carolina, on October 12, 1936. Interestingly, later that same day, The Monroe Brothers recorded it, but called it "The Old Crossroad." Among the later groups to record it were The Blue Sky Boys, Ray and Ina Patterson, and The Stanley Brothers.

There are many paths through this world of sin,
But there's only one I shall travel in;
'Tis the old Cross Road, or the way called "Straight,"
There is just one way to the pearly gate. (Chorus)

    There is just one way (there is just one way)
    To the pearly gate (to the pearly gate),
    To the crown of life (to the crown of life)
    And the friends who wait (and the friends who wait),
    'Tis the old Cross Road ('tis the old Cross Road)
    Or the way called "Straight" (or the way called "Straight"),
    There is just one way (there is just one way)
    To the pearly gate (to the pearly gate).

There are some who sneer at the old Cross Road,
At the pearly gate, and the soul's abode;
Yet I mind them not, but with happy song
Of assurance sweet, still I press along. (Chorus)

Others risk their souls on some new-made way
Thinking they will come to the gate someday;
Oh, may they find out 'ere their lives are done
That the old Cross Road is the only one. (Chorus)

Just Over in the Gloryland

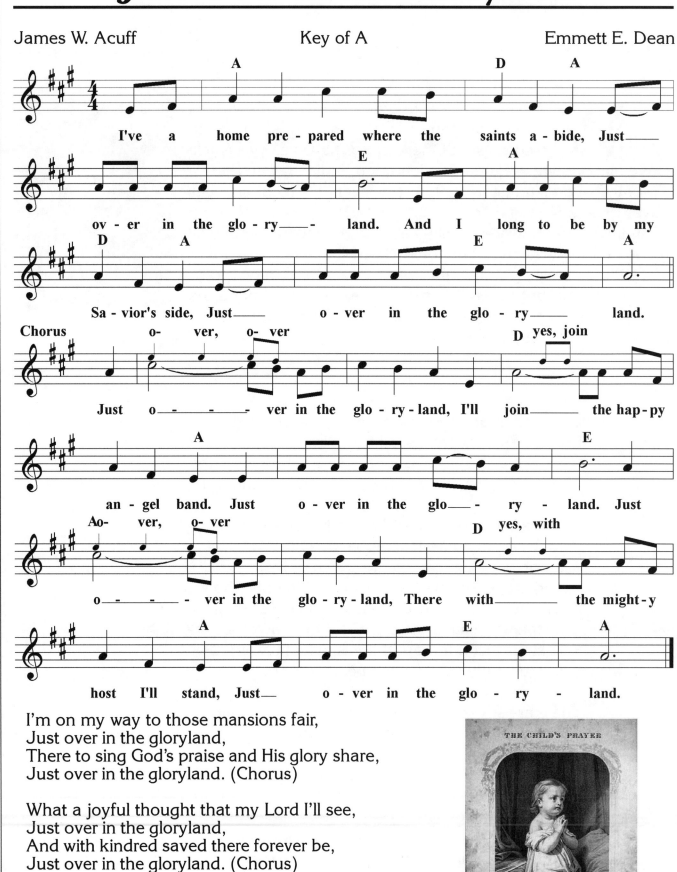

1906

James W. Acuff   Key of A   Emmett E. Dean

I'm on my way to those mansions fair,
Just over in the gloryland,
There to sing God's praise and His glory share,
Just over in the gloryland. (Chorus)

What a joyful thought that my Lord I'll see,
Just over in the gloryland,
And with kindred saved there forever be,
Just over in the gloryland. (Chorus)

With the bloodwashed throng I will shout and sing,
Just over in the gloryland,
Glad hosannas to Christ, the Lord and King,
Just over in the gloryland. (Chorus)

Keep on the Sunny Side of Life 1899

Ada Blenkhorn   Key of G   J. Howard Entwisle

There's a dark and a troub-led side of life, There's a bright and a sun-ny side, too, Though we meet with the dark-ness and strife The sun-ny side we al-so may view.

Chorus

Keep on the sun-ny side, al-ways on the sun-ny side, Keep on the sun-ny side of life, It will help us ev-'ry day it will bright-en all the way, if we keep on the sun-ny side of life.

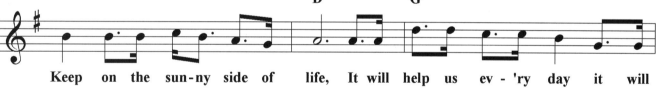

Though the storm in its fury break today,
Crushing hopes that we cherished so dear,
Storm and cloud will in time pass away,
The sun again will shine bright and clear.

Let us greet with a song of hope each day,
Though the moments be cloudy or fair,
Let us trust in our Savior alway,
Who keepeth every one in His care.

"Keep on The Sunny Side." A.P. Carter's epitaph

Kneel at the Cross

Charles E. Moody

Key of G

Charles E. Moody

Kneel at the cross, Christ will meet you there, Come while He waits for you,

List to His voice, Leave with Him your care, And be - gin life a - new.

Chorus

Kneel— at the cross,— Leave— ev - 'ry care,—

Kneel— at the cross,— Je - sus will meet you there.—

Kneel at the cross,
There is room for all,
Who would His glory share,
Bliss there awaits,
Harm can 'er befall,
Those are anchored there. (Chorus)

Kneel at the cross,
Give your idols up,
Look unto realms above,
Turn not away,
To life's sparking cup,
Trust only in His love. (Chorus)

Photo by Lyntha Eiler

Bible at Laurel Glen Regular Baptist Church

102

Charles E. Moody

Charles E. Moody was not your average gospel songwriter. He alone wrote both the words and the melody of two of the bedrock classics of country gospel, "Kneel at the Cross" and "Drifting Too Far From the Shore." To get a handle on this man and the songs he wrote, let's go back to Moody's beginnings in rural Georgia.

One of eight children, Moody was born in a log cabin on October 8, 1891, near Tifton, Georgia. In this rural farming community, music was a favorite pastime, and as a young man Moody learned to play the harmonica and banjo. Later he acquired a fiddle, which he had traded for a shotgun.

Determined to learn to read music, Moody pored over a book of the rudiments of music published by the A. J. Showalter Company of Dalton, Georgia. In 1916, he attended his first singing school in Ebenezer, Georgia, taught by A. J. Simms. There he began learning to sing harmony. Later that year, Moody traveled by train to Asheville, North Carolina, where he learned to sing shaped notes at the Southern Development Normal Music School that had been founded by F.L. Eiland.

Back in Georgia, Moody thoroughly immersed himself in music, singing in quartets, performing at revivals and directing the choirs at churches in the area near his north Georgia home. One day on his way home, he attended a church service led by the Reverend Sam Hair. At the end of his sermon, Reverend Hair asked his congregation to "kneel at the cross." This phrase so struck Moody that the following day he composed the words and music to the now famous gospel song. He soon sent it to George Sebren of The Sebren Music Co, who published it in 1924.

Georgia Yellow Hammers

Unlike most other gospel songwriters, Charles E. Moody also performed and recorded secular music. He joined forces with Bill Chitwood, George Oscar "Bud" Landress, Phil Reeve, and Clyde Evans, and the band was soon calling themselves The Georgia Yellow Hammers. Besides singing in the band, Moody played guitar, banjo and ukulele. He contributed one of his compositions, "Song of the Doodle Bug," which they recorded February 21, 1928.

"Kneel at the Cross," Moody's most popular composition, has appeared in at least 56 songbooks and has been recorded by such diverse artists as The Blue Sky Boys, The Chuck Wagon Gang, Stonewall Jackson, Webb Pierce, The Stanley Brothers, Jim & Jesse, Red Foley, and The Louvin Brothers.

> *"I remember Sunday school and 'Kneel At The Cross' and trying to imagine what God looked like."* Charlie Daniels

Leaning on the Everlasting Arms

Elisha A. Hoffman   Key of G   Anthony J. Showalter

Rather than relying on guesswork or, worse, *research*, we have the Rev. Anthony J. Showalter's own words of how he composed "Leaning on the Everlasting Arms" in 1887. "While I was conducting a singing-school at Hartsells, Alabama, I received a letter from two of my former pupils in South Carolina, conveying the sad intelligence that on the same day each of them had buried his wife...I tried to console them by writing a letter that might prove helpful in their hour of sadness. Among other Scriptures, I quoted the passage, 'Underneath are the everlasting arms.'" This passage so inspired Showalter that he sat down and composed the words and melody to this now-famous hymn. He then sent the manuscript to Elisha A. Hoffman, who completed the poem. Hoffman, no slouch at composing songs himself, was the author of over two thousands gospel songs, including his 1878 gospel classic, "Are You Washed in the Blood of the Lamb."

What a fel - low - ship, what a joy di - vine, Lean - ing on the ev - er - last - ing arms;_____ What a bless - ed - ness, what a peace is mine, Lean - ing on the ev - er - last - ing_____ arms._____

Chorus
Lean - ing, lean - - - ing, Safe and se - cure from all a - larms._____ Lean - ing, lean - ing, Lean - ing on the ev - er - last - ing_____ arms._____

What have I to dread, what have I to fear,
Leaning on the everlasting arms?
I have blessed peace with my Lord so near,
Leaning on the everlasting arms. (Chorus)

Oh how sweet to walk in the pilgrim's way,
Leaning on the everlasting arms;
Oh how bright the path grows from day to day,
Leaning on the everlasting arms. (Chorus)

Let the Church Go Rolling On

Key of G

Even before The Carter Family recorded their influential version of the song they called "Let the Church Roll On" for Victor records on May 25, 1931, the song had been recorded by numerous Black gospel groups including Norfolk Jubilee Quartet (10/1926), Mt. Zion Baptist Quartet of Mobile (3/09/27), The Thankful Quartet (03/17/27), Primitive Baptist Choir of North Carolina (03/26/30), and The Cornfed Four (11/06/30). The Carter Family apparently learned many of the gospel songs they recorded from a religious sect known as Holy Rollers, and that may be where they learned this song. The Carters changed some of the lyrics and turned it into a humorous novelty song that was later recorded by Flatt & Scruggs. Perhaps sensing the song's Black roots, on the Flatt & Scruggs version, Earl laid down his banjo and played it on the guitar in a fingerpicking blues style. This version was collected in the 1920s by Dorothy G. Bolton and published in 1929 in the *Old Songs Hymnal*.

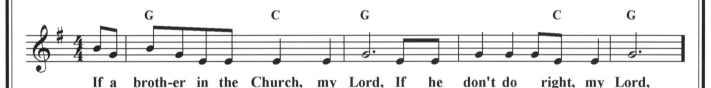

If a broth-er in the Church, my Lord, If he don't do right, my Lord,

Just turn him out, my Lord, And let the Church go a-roll-ing on.

If a sister in the Church, my Lord,
If she don't do right, my Lord,
Just turn her out, my Lord,
And let the Church go a-rolling on.

If a leader in the church, my Lord,
And he don't do right my Lord,
Just turn him out, my Lord,
And let the Church go a-rolling on.

If a liar in the church, my Lord,
And he don't do right my Lord,
Just turn him out, my Lord,
And let the Church go a-rolling on.

If a gambler in the church, my Lord,
And he don't do right my Lord,
Just turn him out, my Lord,
And let the Church go a-rolling on.

Let the Lower Lights Be Burning

P.P. Bliss   Key of G   P.P. Bliss

As a barefoot boy growing up on a farm or lumber camp in Clearfield County, Pennsylvania, Philip Paul Bliss (1838-1876) always loved music. When he was a lad of ten he heard a piano for the first time. Following the music, he impulsively entered a house, bare feet and all, so he could see what was making such a magical sound. The young lady seated at the piano must have thought the poor young farm boy rude for entering her house without first knocking, and quickly dispatched him. Even after working as a sawmill operator and assistant lumber camp cook Bliss's passion for music remained fully ignited. During the Civil War he was hired to teach singing-schools by the legendary songwriter and publisher George F. Root, composer of "Battle Cry of Freedom."

Philip Paul Bliss

Bliss wrote "Let the Lower Lights Be Burning" in 1871 after listening to a sermon preached by the evangelist Dwight L. Moody. That same year, Bliss composed "Almost Persuaded," which became one of the most popular hymns of all time. Bliss' career was cut short when he died in a train wreck on December 29, 1876.

Dark the night of sin has settled,
Loud the angry billows roar;
Eager eyes are watching, longing,
For the lights along the shore. (Chorus)

Trim your feeble lamp, my brother!
Some poor seaman, tempest tossed,
Trying now to make the harbor,
In the darkness may be lost. (Chorus)

Life's Railway to Heaven

M.E. Abbey   Key of D   Charles D. Tillman

This song began as a poem by the Civil War era songsmith William S. Hays, who is best known as the composer of "Little Log Cabin in the Lane," and "The Drummer Boy of Shiloh." Hays' poem entered the folk tradition and was used as the basis of this new song with lyrics by M.E. Abbey and music by Atlanta music publisher Charles D. Tillman.

Life is like a moun-tain rail-road, With an en-gi-neer that's brave, We must make the run suc-cess-ful, From the cra-dle to the grave; Watch the curves, the fills, the tun-nel, Ne-ver fal-ter, ne-ver fail, Keep your hand up-on the throt-tle, And your eye up-on the rail. Bless-ed Sav-ior, Thou will guide us, 'Til we reach that bliss-ful shore, Where the an-gels wait to join us, In Thy praise for-ev-er more.

You will roll up grades of trial, you will cross the bridge of strife,
See that Christ is your conductor on the lightning train of life;
Always mindful of obstruction, do your duty, never fail,
Keep your hand upon the throttle and your eye upon the rail. (Chorus)

You will often find obstructions; look for storms of wind and rain,
On a fill or curve or trestle they will almost ditch your train;
Put your trust alone in Jesus, never falter, never fail,
Keep your hand upon the throttle and your eye upon the rail. (Chorus)

As you roll across the trestle, spanning Jordan's swelling tide,
You behold the union depot into which your train will glide;
There you'll meet the superintendent, God the Father, God the Son,
With the hearty joyous plaudit, "weary pilgrim, welcome home." (Chorus)

Little Moses

Key of G

Mac Wiseman

Although widely known as "a Carter Family song," "Little Moses" is actually much older than the Carter's version. It was arranged around 1871 by G.R. Street and published in 1887 in *Zion Songster #2* by Ruebush, Kieffer & Co. The Carter Family were the first to record it, on February 14, 1929. The diverse list of musicians who have since recorded "Little Moses" includes Roy Acuff, Joan Baez, Ralph Stanley, Laura Boosinger, E.C. and Orna Ball, The Roan Mountain Hilltoppers, The New Lost City Ramblers, and Mac Wiseman. This version is the one that was first published in 1887.

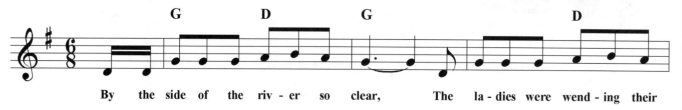

By the side of the riv-er so clear, The la-dies were wend-ing their

way; As Pha-ra-oh's daught-er stepped down to the wa-ter to

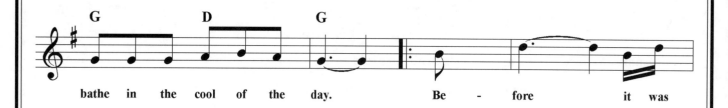

bathe in the cool of the day. Be - fore it was

dark she o-pened the ark, And found the sweet in-fant was there.

Little Moses

By the side of the river so clear,
The ladies were wending their way;
As Pharaoh's daughter stepped down to the water
To bathe in the cool of the day.

Before it was dark she opened the ark
And found the sweet infant was there.

By the side of the river so clear,
The infant was lonely and sad;
She took him in pity, and thought him so pretty,
And made little Moses so glad.

She called him her own, her beautiful son,
And sent for a nurse that was near.

Then away by the river so clear,
They carried that beautiful child;
To his own tender mother, his sister and brother,
Then Moses looked happy and smiled.

His mother, so good, done all that she could,
To rear him and teach him with care.

Then away by the sea that was red,
Stood Moses the servant of God,
While in him confided the deep was divided,
As upward he lifted his rod.
The Jews safely crossed while Pharaoh's host,
Was drowned in the waters and lost.

The Jews safely crossed while Pharaoh's host,
Was drowned in the waters and lost.

Then away on the mountain so high,
The last one he ever might see,
While Israel victorious, his hope was most glorious,
Would soon over Jordan be free.

Then his labors did cease, he departed in peace,
And rests in the heaven above.

New Salem Regular Baptist Church, Allegheny County, NC

109

The Lone Pilgrim

Attributed to Richard Keen   Key of G   Anonymous

I came to the place where the lone pil-grim lay,

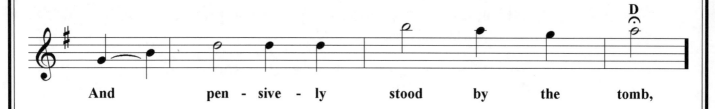

And pen - sive - ly stood by the tomb,

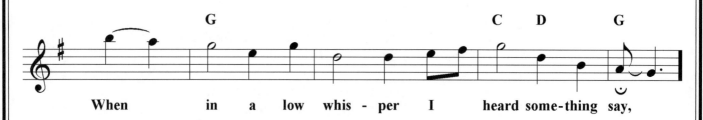

When in a low whis - per I heard some-thing say,

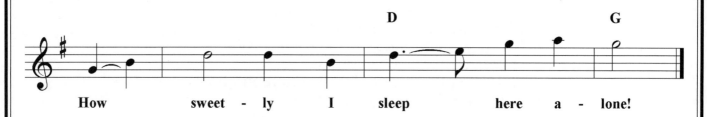

How sweet - ly I sleep here a - lone!

The tempest may howl, and the loud thunder roar,
And gathering storms may arise,
Yet calm is my feeling, at rest is my soul,
The tears are all wiped from my eyes.

The cause of my Master compelled me from home,
I bade my companion farewell;
I blessed my dear children, who now for me mourn,
In far distant regions they dwell.

I wandered an exile and stranger from home,
No kindred or relative nigh;
I met the contagion, and sank to the tomb,
My soul flew to mansions on high.

Oh tell my companion and children most dear,
To weep not for me now I'm gone;
The same hand that led me through scenes most severe,
Has kindly assisted me home.

Lord, I'm Coming Home

William J. Kirkpatrick   Key of A   William J. Kirkpatrick

William J. Kirkpatrick was a nineteenth-century music teacher and composer, but he was best known as an editor and compiler of Sunday school and gospel hymnbooks. Along with John R. Sweeney, in 1878 he founded The Praise Publishing Company, which helped to popularize gospel music. Together, Kirkpatrick and Sweeney published some fifty songbooks which sold several million copies. After Sweeney's death, Kirkpatrick knocked off another fifty songbooks on his own.

The Callahan Brothers

He composed the words and music to "Lord, I'm Coming Home" in 1892. It was recorded on August 16, 1934, by The Callahan Brothers along with their sister, Alma.

I've wand-ered far a-way from God, Now I'm com-ing home; The paths of sin too long I've trod, Lord, I'm com-ing home. Com-ing home, com-ing home, Nev-er more to roam; O-pen wide thine arms of love, Lord, I'm com-ing home.

I've wasted many precious years,
Now I'm coming home;
I now repent with bitter tears,
Lord, I'm coming home. (Chorus)

I'm tired of sin and straying, Lord,
Now I'm coming home;
I'll trust Thy love, believe Thy word,
Lord, I'm coming home. (Chorus)

My soul is sick, my heart is sore,
Now I'm coming home;
My strength renew, my hope restore,
Lord, I'm coming home. (Chorus)

My only hope, my only plea,
Now I'm coming home;
That Jesus died, and died for me,
Lord, I'm coming home. (Chorus)

Methodist Pie

Key of D

I was down to camp meet-in' The oth-er af-ter-noon to
2. (There's) old Un-cle Dan-iel, And Bro-ther Eb-e-ne-zer,

hear them shout and sing, For to tell each oth-er how they
with his lame gal, Sue, Aunt Pol-ly and Me-lin-da, And

love one an-oth-er; And to make hal-le-lu-jah ring. There's
old Mo-ther Ben-der, Well, I nev-er seen a hap-pi-er

crew. Oh, lit-tle chil-dren, I be-lieve,

Oh, lit-tle chil-dren I be-lieve, Oh, lit-tle chil-dren

I be-lieve, I'm a Meth-od-ist 'til I die, I'm a

Meth-od-ist, a Meth-od-ist, 'Tis my be-lief, Meth-od-ist 'til I die, When

old grim death comes a knock-in' at the door, I'm a Meth-od-ist 'til I die.

Methodist Pie

Bradley Kincaid, the "Kentucky Mountain Boy," was the first to record this good-natured song. It was so popular that Kincaid actually recorded it three times, first on February 27, 1927, and then in 1929 and 1930. Gene Autry recorded it in 1931. Kincaid relates that a man wrote it after going to Camp Nelson, Kentucky, to hear circuit riding preachers at old-fashioned Methodist camp meetings.

WLS late 1920s

I was down to camp meetin' the other afternoon to hear them shout and sing,
For to tell each other how they love one another; and to make hallelujah ring.
There's old Uncle Daniel, and Brother Ebenezer, with his lame gal, Sue
Aunt Polly and Melinda and old Mother Bender, well I never seen a happier crew.

    Oh, little children, I believe, Oh little children, I believe,
    Oh little children, I believe, I'm a Methodist 'til I die.
    I'm a Methodist, a Methodist, 'tis my belief, Methodist 'til I die,
    When old grim death comes a knocking at the door, I'm a Methodist 'till I die.

Well, they all go there for to have a good time, and to eat that grub so sly,
Have applesauce butter with sugar in the gourd, and a great big Methodist pie.
Well, you ought to hear the ringing when they all get to singing, that good old "Bye and Bye,"
See Jimmy McGee in the top of a tree, saying "How is this for high?" (Chorus)

Then they catch a hold of hands and march around the ring, kept a-singing all the while,
You'd think it was a cyclone coming through the air, you can hear them shout a half a mile.
Then the bell rings loud and the great big crowd, breaks ranks and up they fly,
While I took board on the sugar in the gourd, and I cleaned up the Methodist pie. (Chorus)

Courtesy of Barbara Swell

My Old Cottage Home

R. A. Glenn   Key of G   R. A. Glenn

I am think-ing to-night of my old cot-tage home, That stands on the brow of the hill, Where in

life's ear-ly morn-ing I once loved to roam, But now all is qui-et and still. Oh my

Chorus

old cot-tage home, my old cot-tage home, Stand-ing down by the hill, Where in

life's ear-ly morn-ing I once loved to roam, But now all is qui-et and still.

Many years have gone by since in prayer there I knelt,
With dear ones around the old hearth,
But my mother's sweet prayers in my heart still are felt,
I'll treasure them here while on earth. (Chorus)

One by one they have gone from the old cottage home,
On earth I shall see them no more,
But with them I shall meet 'round the beautiful throne,
Where parting will come never more! (Chorus)

Oh! Those Tombs

William M. Golden   Key of E   William M. Golden

William M. Golden, who also composed "A Beautiful Life," and "Where the Soul Never Dies," wrote this hymn in the late 1880s. The Blue Sky Boys learned it from their father's old shaped-note hymnal that bore this chilling note: "composed after a walk through the city of the dead." It was recorded by Wade Mainer & Sons of the Mountaineer in Charlotte, North Carolina, on January 27, 1938 and on November 7, 1938 by Roy Hall and His Blue Ridge Entertainers. It often goes by the name "Lonely Tombs."

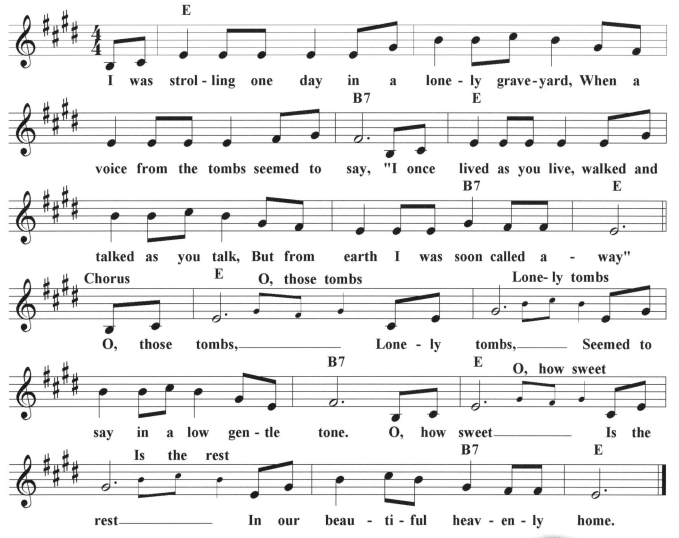

I was strol - ling one day in a lone - ly grave-yard, When a voice from the tombs seemed to say, "I once lived as you live, walked and talked as you talk, But from earth I was soon called a - way"

Chorus O, those tombs, Lone - ly tombs, Seemed to say in a low gen - tle tone. O, how sweet Is the rest In our beau - ti - ful heav - en - ly home.

Every voice from the tombs seemed to whisper and say,
"Living man, you must soon follow me,"
And I thought as I looked at these cold marble slabs,
What a dark, lonely place that must be. (Chorus)

Then I came to the place where my mother was laid,
And in silence I stood by her tomb,
And her voice seemed to say in a low, gentle tone,
"I am safe with my Savior at home." (Chorus)

The Old Account Was Settled

When this song was written in 1905 by F.M. Graham, it was still common practice to keep a tab at the general store where you settled your account once a month, or whenever you could. It was first recorded by Frank Welling and John McGhee in Ashland, Kentucky, on February 12, 1928. The Blue Sky Boys recorded it in Charlotte, North Carolina, on October 13, 1936.

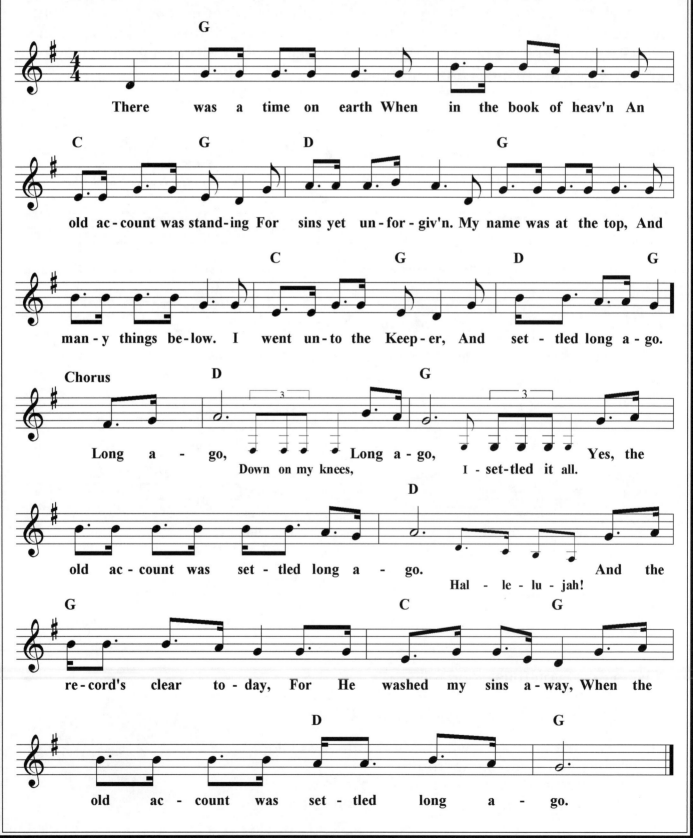

The Old Account Was Settled

F.M. Graham   Key of G   F.M. Graham

There was a time on earth when in the book of heaven
An old account was standing for sins yet unforgiven.
My name was at the top, and many things below.
I went unto the Keeper, and settled long ago.

Long ago (down on my knees), Long ago, (I settled it all).
Yes the old account was settled long ago. (Hallelujah!)
And the record's clear today, for He washed my sins away,
When the old account was settled long ago.

The old account was large, and growing every day;
For I was always sinning, and never tried to pay.
But when I looked ahead, and saw such pain and woe,
I said that I would settle, I settled long ago. (Chorus)

When at the judgment bar I stand before my King,
And He the book will open, He cannot find a thing.
Then will my heart be glad, while tears of joy will flow
Because I had it settled, and settled long ago. (Chorus)

When in that happy home, my Savior's home above,
I'll sing redemption's story, and praise Him for His love;
I'll not forget that book, with pages white as snow,
Because I came and settled, and settled long ago. (Chorus)

O sinner, seek the Lord, repent of all your sin,
For thus He hath commanded, if you would enter in.
And then if you should live a hundred years below,
Up there you'll not regret it, you settled long ago. (Chorus)

Photo by Wayne Erbsen

The Old Gospel Ship

Key of D

Although the composer of "The Old Gospel Ship" remains a mystery, this very old song gained wide popularity as recorded by The Carter Family in New York City on May 7, 1935. Folklorist Gus Meade has pointed out in his book *Country Music Sources* that the melody is identical to that of "Feast Here Tonight," which was first recorded by the Prairie Ramblers and seems to have roots going back to the African-American folk tradition in the days before the Civil War. It's been recorded by a diverse list of musicians that include The Monroe Brothers, Johnny Cash, Red Smiley and The Bluegrass Cutups, and Joan Baez.

I have good news to bring and that is why I sing; All my joys with you I'll share; I'm going to take a trip in the Old Gos-pel Ship, And go sail-ing through the air.

Chorus

O I'm gon-na take a trip, in the good Old Gos-pel Ship, I'm go-ing far be-yond the sky; O I'm gon-na shout and sing un-til the hea-vens ring, When I'm bid-ding this world good-bye.

The Old Gospel Ship

I have good news to bring, and that is why I sing,
All my joys with you I'll share;
I'm going to take a trip in the Old Gospel Ship
And go sailing through the air.

O I'm going to take a trip, in the Old Gospel Ship,
I'm going far beyond the sky;
O I'm gonna shout and sing until the heavens ring,
When I'm bidding this world goodbye.

I can scarcely wait, I know I won't be late,
I'll spend my time in prayer;
And when the ship comes in, I'll leave this world of sin
And go sailing through the air. (Chorus)

If you are ashamed of me, you ought not to be.
Yes, you'd better have a care;
If too much fault you find, you will sure be left behind
While I'm sailing through the air. (Chorus)

The Old Rugged Cross

Rev. George Bennard   Key of G   Rev. George Bennard

On a hill far a - way stood an old rug - ged cross, The
em - blem of suf - f'ring and shame, And I love that old cross where the
dear - est and best for a world of lost sin - ners was slain.

Chorus

So I'll cher - ish the old rug - ged cross, Till my
cross, the old rug - ged cross,
tro - phies at last I lay down; I will cling to the old - rug - ged cross
the
cross, And ex - change it some day for a crown.
old rug - ged cross,

Church Etiquette: Don't, if you go to a strange church, decline to contribute to the offertory on the grounds that you do not like the service. (1884)

The Old Rugged Cross

Few songs have managed to be as popular as "The Old Rugged Cross" both with those who love hymns as well as those who love old secular songs. It was composed in 1913 in Michigan by George Bennard (1873-1958), who was born in Youngstown, Ohio. When he was sixteen, his father passed away, so Bennard found work with the Salvation Army. He was later ordained as a minister in Methodist Episcopal Church. Bennard explained how he came to write the hymn.

"The inspiration came to me one day in 1913, when I was staying in Albion, Michigan. I began to write "The Old Rugged Cross." I composed the melody first. The words that I first wrote were imperfect. The words of the finished hymn were put into my heart in answer to my own need. Shortly thereafter it was introduced at special meetings in Pokagon, Michigan, on June 7, 1913. The first occasion where it was heard outside of the church at Pokagon was at the Chicago Evangelistic Institute. There it was introduced before a large convention and soon it became extremely popular throughout the country."

On a hill far away stood an old rugged cross,
The emblem of suffering and shame,
And I love that old cross where the dearest and best,
For a world of lost sinners was slain.

So I'll cherish the old rugged cross,
Till my trophies at last I lay down;
I will cling to the old rugged cross,
And exchange it some day for a crown.

Oh, that old rugged cross, so despised by the world,
Has a wondrous attraction for me,
For the dear Lamb of God left His glory above,
To bear it to dark Calvary. (Chorus)

In the old rugged cross, stained with blood so divine,
A wondrous beauty I see,
For 'twas on that old cross Jesus suffered and died,
To pardon and sanctify me. (Chorus)

To the old rugged cross I will ever be true,
Its shame and reproach gladly bear;
Then He'll call me some day to my home far away,
Where His glory forever I'll share. (Chorus)

Old-Time Religion

Key of G

What makes "Old-Time Religion" so popular is that it is so easy to sing. The verse and the chorus have the same melody, and there is little variation between the verses, so it is easy to remember. It was first recorded by Ernest Thompson in New York City on May 4, 1927.

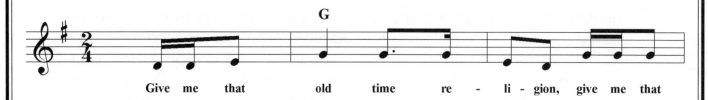

Give me that old time re - li - gion, give me that

old time re - li - gion, give me that old time re -

li - gion, It's good e - nough for me.

Turtle Island Preserve, Triplett, NC

Photo by Wayne Erbsen

Old-Time Religion

Photo by David Holt

Quay Smathers

Give me that old time religion,
Give me that old time religion,
Give me that old time religion,
It's good enough for me.

It was good for Paul and Silas,
It was good for Paul and Silas,
It was good for Paul and Silas,
It's good enough for me. (Chorus)

It was good for our mothers,
It was good for our mothers,
It was good for our mothers,
It's good enough for me. (Chorus)

Makes me love everybody,
Makes me love everybody,
Makes me love everybody,
It's good enough for me. (Chorus)

It was precious to our fathers,
It was precious to our fathers,
It was precious to our fathers,
It's good enough for me. (Chorus)

It will take us all to heaven,
It will take us all to heaven,
It will take us all to heaven,
It's good enough for me. (Chorus)

On the Sea of Life

George W. Sebren   Key of G   T.S. Sloan

We are on the sea of life, Sail-ing to a bet-ter home, Where the
saved of all the earth now a - bide, Leav-ing all our tri-als here, Man-y
plea-sures wait us there when we've crossed the foam and reached the oth - er side.

Chorus
Sail - - - - - - - - - - ing
We are sail - ing on-ward, sail-ing, sail - ing o'er the foam, We are
on, cling-ing to our Cap-tain as the an - gry bil - lows come, Soon, yes,
Sail - - - - - - - - - - - ing
soon we'll reach the har - bor and be safe be - yond the tide, We are
to the oth - er side.
go - ing on - ward to the oth - er side.

124

On the Sea of Life

One of my all time favorite sacred songs, "On The Sea of Life" was composed by George W. Sebren (lyrics) and T.S. Sloan (melody). Although not well known today, Sebren was an important figure in the beginning of gospel music. When James D. Vaughan put together his first quartet in May of 1910, Sebren was hired to sing lead. For that he was paid $50 a month.

My own connection to Sebren happened when researching my first gospel songbook about twenty-five years ago. A friend in my hometown of Asheville, North Carolina, mentioned that her parents' barn was full of old hymn books. Without delay, I went out there and was shocked to find an old wooden shed filled to overflowing with paperback shaped-note gospel songbooks. There were literally thousands of them, all in various stages of decay. Investigating further, I noticed that the title page of many of the books was stamped in bright red: "Send Your Orders to Skyland Book Shop, Asheville, NC, 40 N. Lexington Ave" (see below). I soon found out that in Sebren's later years he opened a religious book shop, and, when he eventually sold his business, the remaining books were left in the leaky old shed where they had remained undisturbed until I happened on them many years later. To me, stumbling on this stash of books was like finding lost treasure, and I spent many happy hours poring over those books.

"On the Sea of Life" was first recorded by Roper's Mountain Singers on November 2, 1927 in Atlanta, Georgia. My favorite recording of the song was by Doyle Lawson & Quicksilver on the classic bluegrass gospel album called "Rock My Soul."

We are on the sea of life sailing to a better home,
Where the saved of all the earth now abide;
Leaving all our trials here, many pleasures wait us there,
When we've crossed the foam and reached the other side.

   Sail - (We are sailing onward, sailing, sailing o'er the foam, we are) - ing
   On (Clinging to our Captain as the angry billows come; soon yes)
   Sail-(Soon we'll reach the harbor and be safe beyond the tide, we are) - ing
   To (Going onward to) the other side, (the other side).

We've a Captain brave and true,
Who will guide us over the blue,
And will shield us when the storms hover nigh,
He can still the angry wave,
And from evil He can save,
If we'll trust Him and His loving promise try. (Chorus)

Many millions now abide,
In that home beyond the sky,
Where the ransomed pilgrims wait free from care,
There is room on board for all,
Who will heed the Captain's call,
And take ship for heaven's country bright and fair. (Chorus)

125

On the Sunny Side of Life

Tillit S. Teddlie   Key of A   J. Wesley Watts

There are shady dells where no gladness dwells,
And the clouds obstruct the view;
But a brighter way like the light of day,
Is a-waiting there for you. (Chorus)

Let us sing a song as we go along,
Let us banish care and strife,
That the world may know as we onward go,
There's a sunny side of life. (Chorus)

Our Meeting Is Over

Key of G

Fa - thers, now our meet - ing is o - ver, Sure - ly we must part, And if I nev - er see you a - gain I'll love you in my heart. Yes, we'll land on the shore, Yes, we'll land on the shore, Lord, we'll land on the shore and be saved for - ev - er more.

Mothers....

Sisters...

Palms of Victory

John B. Matthias   Key of F   John B. Matthias

Composed in 1836 by John B. Matthias, "Palms of Victory" is also called "Deliverance Will Come," as well as "The Wayworn Traveler." It was published in the 1855 edition of *The Social Harp*. In the 1960s, folksinger Hedy West sang a parody of this song that went "pans of biscuits, bowls of gravy, pans of biscuits, we shall have."

I saw a way-worn trav-'ler, In tat-tered gar-ments clad, And Strug-gling up the moun-tain, It seemed that he was sad. His back was lad-en heav-y, His strength was al-most gone, Yet he shout-ed as he jour-neyed "De-liv-er-ance will come" Then palms of vic-to-ry, Crowns of glo-ry, Palms of vic-to-ry, I shall wear.

Palms of Victory

I saw a wayworn traveler,
In tattered garments clad,
And struggling up the mountain,
It seemed that he was sad.
His back was laden heavy,
His strength was almost gone,
Yet he shouted as he journeyed
"Deliverance will come."

    Then palms of victory, crowns of glory,
    Palms of victory I shall wear.

The summer sun was shining,
The sweat was on his brow,
His garments worn and dusty,
His steps seemed very slow.
But he kept pressing onward,
For he was wending home,
Still shouting as he journeyed
"Deliverance will come." (Chorus)

The songsters in the arbor,
That stood beside the way,
Attracted his attention,
Inviting his delay.
His watchword being "Onward!'
He stopped his ears and ran,
Still shouting as he journeyed
"Deliverance will come." (Chorus)

I saw him in the evening,
The sun was bending low,
He'd overtopped the mountain,
And reached the vale below.
He saw the golden city.
His everlasting home,
And shouted loud "Hosanna,
Deliverance will come!" (Chorus)

While gazing on that city,
Just o'er that narrow flood,
A band of holy angels,
Came from the throne of God.
They bore him on their pinions
Safe o'er the dashing foam,
And joined him in his triumph
Deliverance has come! (Chorus)

I heard the song of triumph,
They sang upon the shore,
Saying, "Jesus has redeemed us,
To suffer nevermore."
Then casting his eyes backward,
On the race which he had run,
He shouted loud "Hosanna,
Deliverance has come!" (Chorus)

Paynes Chapel, Sandy Mush, NC,

Photo by Mary Jo Brezny

Pass Me Not

Fanny J. Crosby   Key of G   William H. Doane

Pass me not, O gen-tle Sav - ior, Hear my hum - ble cry,

while on oth - ers Thou art call - ing, Do not pass me by.

Chorus

Sav - ior, Sav - ior Hear my hum - ble cry,

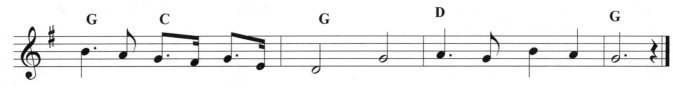

While on oth - ers Thou art call - ing, Do not pass me by.

Let me at a throne of mercy,
Find a sweet relief,
Kneeling there in deep contrition,
Help my unbelief. (Chorus)

Trusting only in Thy merit,
Would I seek Thy face,
Healing my wounded, broken spirit,
Save me by Thy grace. (Chorus)

Thou the Spring of all my comfort,
More than life to me,
Whom have I on earth beside Thee?
Whom in heaven but Thee? (Chorus)

Pass Me Not

Originally entitled "Pass Me Not O Gentle Savior," this classic hymn came to life in 1868 as part of a collaboration between Dr. William Doane and blind poet Fanny J. Crosby. Over the years, their successful partnership produced at least one thousand hymns, with Doane composing the melodies and Crosby writing the lyrics.

Doane actually did his composing as a hobby. In addition to owning a woodworking machinery business, he served as president of several other businesses and was an inventor, holding at least seventy patents. Active as a philanthropist, Doane donated generously to the YMCA, Denison University, and the Cincinnati Art Museum.

Fanny J. Crosby was one of the most gifted poets of the 19th century. Blinded as an infant by an incompetent doctor who was treating her for an eye inflammation in 1835, Crosby studied at the New York Institution for the Blind. By 1847 she had become an instructor at the school. During this period, one of her frequent collaborators was George F. Root, who was a legendary songwriter and publisher of the Civil War era. While Root composed such classics as "The Vacant Chair," "Battle Cry of Freedom," "Just Before the Battle Mother," and "Tramp, Tramp, Tramp," Crosby excelled at writing the lyrics to a large number of hymns. Her enduring compositions included such songs as "Safe in the Arms of Jesus" (1869), "Jesus Keep Me Near the Cross" (1869), as well as "Blessed Assurance" (1873). Although she made enough money writing hymns to support a moderate lifestyle, she chose instead to live in crowded tenement houses and she gave most of her money away. By the time she passed away in 1915 at the age of ninety-five, she had written over nine thousand hymn lyrics and made an indelible mark on gospel music.

Photo by Lyntha Eiler

An elderly woman who was hard of hearing entered a church with an old-fashioned ear trumpet. Soon after she was seated, an usher tiptoed over and whispered, "One toot, and you're outta here!"

Pilgrim of Sorrow

My mother has reached the bright glory,
My father's still walking in sin.
My brothers and sisters won't own me,
Because I am trying to get in. (Chorus)

When friends and relatives forsake me,
And troubles roll 'round me so high,
I think of the kind words of Jesus,
"Poor pilgrim I am always nigh." (Chorus)

Poor Wayfaring Stranger

Key of Am

I am a poor—— way - far - ing stran - ger, While tra - vel - ing through—— this world of woe,—— Yet there's no sick - ness, toil or dan - ger, In that bright world—— to which I go.——

Chorus

I'm go - ing there—— to see my fa - ther, I'm go - ing there—— no more to roam,—— I'm on - ly go - ing o - ver Jor - dan, I'm on - ly go - ing o - ver home.——

I know dark clouds will gather 'round me
I know my way is rough and steep,
Yet beauteous fields lie just before me
Where God's redeemed their vigils keep.

I'm going there to see my mother
She said she'd meet me when I come,
I'm only going over Jordan,
I'm only going over home.

I'll soon be free from every trial
My body sleeps in the churchyard,
I'll drop the cross of self-denial
And enter on my great reward.

I'm going there to see my Savior
To sing His praise forevermore
I'm only going over Jordan,
I'm only going over home.

Power in the Blood

L.E. Jones   Key of G   L.E. Jones

Would you be free from your bur-den of sin? There's pow'r in the blood, pow'r in the blood; Would you o'er e-vil a vic-to-ry win? There is won-der-ful pow'r in the blood.

Chorus

There is pow'r, pow'r, Won-der work-ing pow'r in the
There is pow'r,
blood of the Lamb; There is pow'r, pow'r,
in the blood of the Lamb; there is pow'r
Won-der work-ing pow'r in the pre-cious blood of the Lamb.

Would you be free from your passion and pride?
There's pow'r in the blood, pow'r in the blood,
Come for a cleansing to Calvary's tide,
There's wonderful pow'r in the blood. (Chorus)

Would you be whiter, much whiter than snow?
There's pow'r in the blood, pow'r in the blood,
Sin stains are lost in its life giving flow,
There's wonderful pow'r in the blood. (Chorus)

Would you do service for Jesus your King?
There's pow'r in the blood, pow'r in the blood,
Would you live daily, His praises to sing?
There's wonderful pow'r in the blood. (Chorus)

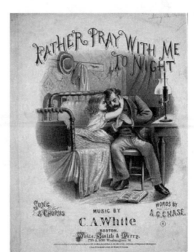

Precious Memories

J.B.F. Wright   Key of G   J.B.F. Wright

Unlike most gospel songwriters, J.B.F. Wright had no formal music training. Born in Tennessee on February 21, 1877, Wright wrote solely from inspiration. As he once explained it, "The words come spontaneously, flowing into place when I feel the divine urge." The list of artists who have recorded this gospel classic goes on and on and includes the likes of Boxcar Willie, Roy Acuff, Bill Anderson, Chet Atkins, The Blackwood Brothers, Johnny Cash, Jimmy Dean, Duane Eddy, Tennessee Ernie Ford, Aretha Franklin, Merle Haggard, Andy Griffith, Bill Monroe, The Jordanaires, George Jones, and Ray Price.

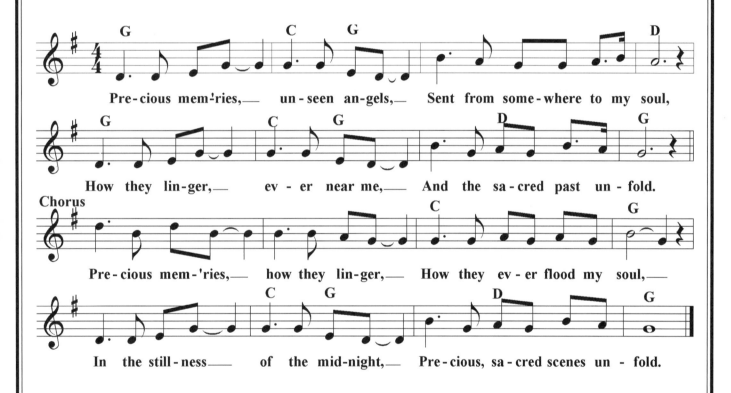

Pre-cious mem-'ries,— un-seen an-gels,— Sent from some-where to my soul,

How they lin-ger,— ev - er near me,— And the sa-cred past un - fold.

Chorus

Pre-cious mem-'ries,— how they lin-ger,— How they ev - er flood my soul,—

In the still-ness—— of the mid-night,— Pre-cious, sa-cred scenes un - fold.

Precious father, loving mother
Fly across the lonely years
And old home scenes of my childhood
In fond memory appears. (Chorus)

In the stillness of the midnight
Echoes from the past I hear
Old-time singing, gladness bringing
From that lovely land somewhere. (Chorus)

As I travel on life's pathway
Knowing not what the years may hold
As I ponder, hope grows fonder
Precious mem'ries flood my soul. (Chorus)

135

Row Us Over the Tide

E.C. Avis   Key of D   E.C. Avis

For those who love sentimental songs, here is a real gem. It was recorded by The Blue Sky Boys in their first Bluebird session on June 15, 1936. The transcription below is from the recording made by Kelly Harrell & Henry Norton with the Virginia String Band, August 8, 1927 for RCA Victor.

Two lit - tle chil - dren were strol - ling one day down by the

lone ri - ver side. One stepped up to the

boat - man and said, "Row us o - ver the tide."

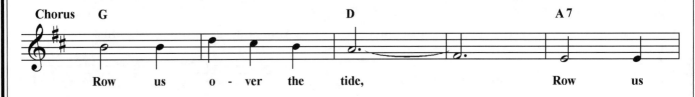

Chorus   Row us o - ver the tide, Row us

o - ver the tide, One stepped up to the

boat - man and said, "Row us o - ver the tide."

Be kind to us, mister, dear mother is dead
We have no place to abide.
Our father's a gambler and cares not for us,
Please row us over the tide. (Chorus)

Papa and mama so weary one day
Said "Jesus would come for their child."
We are so tired of waiting so long,
Please row us over the tide. (Chorus)

The angels took mother to her heavenly home
There with the saints to abide.
Now father has forsaken us, he's left us alone,
Please row us over the tide. (Chorus)

The Royal Telephone

Frederick M. Lehman   Key of C   Frederick M. Lehman

With the growing popularity of the telephone in the first decade of the twentieth century, it was no surprise when the gadget entered popular culture through music. Other telephone songs from this period included "Hello Central, Give Me Heaven" and "Ring Me Up Heaven." "The Royal Telephone" was recorded by Mac and Bob, The Morris Brothers, The Blue Sky Boys, Wade Mainer, and Carl Story.

Central's never "busy", al-ways on the line, you may hear from heav-en Al-most an-y time.

'Tis a roy-al serv-ice, free for one and all - when you get in trou-ble give this roy-al line a call.

Chorus

Tel - e-phone to glo-ry, O what joy di-vine! I can feel the cur-rent mov-ing on the line;

Built by God the Father for His loved and own, We may talk to Je-sus thro' this roy-al tel-e-phone.

There will be no charges, telephone is free;
It was built for service, just for you and me.
There will be no waiting on this royal line
Telephone to glory always answers just in time. (Chorus)

Fail to get the answer, Satan's crossed your wire
By some strong delusion, or some base desire.
Take away obstructions, God is on the throne
And you'll get the answer through this royal telephone. (Chorus)

If your line is "grounded," and connection true
Has been lost with Jesus, tell you what to do:
Prayer and faith and promise mend the broken wire,
Till your soul is burning with the Pentecostal fire. (Chorus)

Carnal combinations cannot get control
Of this line to glory, anchored in the soul.
Storm and trial cannot disconnect the line
Held in constant keeping by the Father's hand divine. (Chorus)

Shake Hands With Mother Again

W.A. Berry   Key of G   W.A. Berry

Mother songs have always been popular with old-time country and blue-grass musicians and fans alike. "Shake Hands With Mother Again" was first recorded on December 19, 1930, by The Central Mississippi Quartet. Those who also recorded it include Asher Sizemore and Little Jimmy, Bill Cox, The Carolina Buddies, and Wade Mainer & Zeke Morris. It's been recorded in bluegrass style by Red Allen and Jimmy Martin.

If I should be liv-ing when Je-sus comes, And
know the day and the hour, I'd like to be stand-ing at
When I can hear Je-sus my
moth-er's tomb, When Je-sus comes in His power.
Sav-ior say, "Shake hands with moth-er a-gain."

Chorus
T'will be a won-der-ful hap-py day, Up there in the gol-den strand,

I'd like to say, "Mother, this is your boy
You left when you went away
And now my dear mother, it gives me great joy
To see you again today." (Chorus)

There's coming a time when I can go home
To meet my loved ones there
There I can see Jesus upon His throne
In that bright city so fair. (Chorus)

There'll be no sorrow no pain to bear
In that home beyond the sky
A glorious thought when we all get there
We never will say "goodbye." (Chorus)

Shall We Gather at the River?

Robert Lowry   Key of D   Robert Lowry

A pastor with spellbinding oratory skills, Robert Lowry wrote religious songs that often had appeal far beyond the church house walls. Among the many songs he wrote were "Where is My Wandering Boy Tonight," "I Need Three Every Hour," and "Nothing But the Blood." Lowry's inspiration to write "Shall We Gather at the River?" occurred in the hot summer of 1864 while he was a Baptist minister in New York City. When an epidemic claimed countless lives, Lowry assured many of the living that they would meet their loved ones "at the river of life that flowed by the throne of God." He composed this song while seated at the organ late one afternoon. It was one of the favorite songs of Uncle Dave Macon.

Shall we gath-er at the riv - er, Where bright an-gel feet have trod;——

With its crys-tal tide for - ev - er, Flow-ing by the throne of—— God?

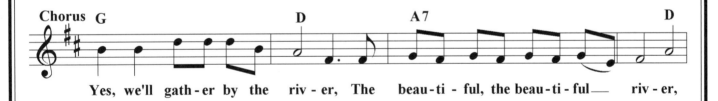

Chorus
Yes, we'll gath-er by the riv - er, The beau-ti - ful, the beau-ti-ful—— riv - er,

Gath-er with the saints at the riv - er, That flows by the throne of—— God.

On the margin of the river,
Washing up its silver spray,
We will walk and worship ever,
All the happy golden day. (Chorus)

There we reach the shining river,
Lay we every burden down,
Grace our spirits will deliver,
And provide a robe and crown. (Chorus)

Soon we'll reach the shining river,
Soon our pilgrimage will cease,
Soon our happy hearts will quiver,
With the melody of peace. (Chorus)

Standing in the Need of Prayer

Key of G

Standing in the Need of Prayer

Although the composer of "Standing in the Need of Prayer" will never be known, the song appears to have been inspired by the camp meeting revivals which started in Kentucky as early as 1800. Its simple words and call and response style on the chorus make it a natural to sing with an audience unfamiliar with the song. It was first recorded by John & Emery McClung's West Virginia Snake Hunters in New York City on March 7, 1927.

Not my brother, nor my sister, but it's me, O Lord,
Standing in the need of prayer;
Not my brother, nor my sister, but it's me, O Lord,
Standing in the need of prayer.

It's me, (it's me) it's me, O Lord,
Standing in the need of prayer;
It's me, (it's me) it's me, O Lord,
Standing in the need of prayer;

Not the preacher, nor the deacon, but it's me, O Lord,
Standing in the need of prayer;
Not the preacher, nor the deacon, but it's me, O Lord,
Standing in the need of prayer. (Chorus)

Not my father, nor my mother, but it's me, O Lord,
Standing in the need of prayer;
Not my father, nor my mother, but it's me, O Lord,
Standing in the need of prayer. (Chorus)

Not the stranger, nor my neighbor, but it's me, O Lord,
Standing in the need of prayer;
Not the stranger, nor my neighbor, but it's me, O Lord.
Standing in the need of prayer. (Chorus)

Swing Low Sweet Chariot

Key of G

Few gospel songs have ever approached the widespread popularity of this old Black spiritual. It was first performed publicly by The Fisk Jubilee Singers of Fisk University of Nashville, Tennessee, and published in their book *Jubilee Songs*, which was copyrighted March 11, 1872.

I looked o - ver Jor - dan and what did I see,— Com - ing for to car - ry me home? A band of an - gels com - ing af - ter me,— Com - ing for to car - ry me home.

Chorus

Swing— low, sweet char - i - ot,— Com - ing for to car - ry me home, Swing— low, sweet char - i - ot,— com - ing for to car - ry me home.

142

Swing Low Sweet Chariot

I'm sometimes up, I'm sometimes down,
Coming for to carry me home,
But still my soul is heavenly bound,
Coming for to carry me home. (Chorus)

If you get there before I do,
Coming for to carry me home,
Tell all my friends that I'm comin' too,
Coming for to carry me home. (Chorus)

I've never been to heaven, but I been told,
Coming for to carry me home,
The streets of heaven are paved with gold,
Coming for to carry me home.

In the years before the Civil War, it was illegal to teach slaves to read or to write. All that changed with the winning of the war and the emancipation of the slaves. Hungry for an education, some newly freed slaves eventually made their way to Fisk University in Nashville, Tennessee, which began accepting students in 1866. One of Fisk's first teachers was a young white man named George L. White, who began teaching music to a number of gifted students. Struck by the passion for their own music, White built on his students' musical strengths and allowed them to sing the spirituals they had grown up with. In 1867, White's group made their first public performance in Nashville. They were so well received that in 1871, White hit upon the idea of setting up a tour as a way to raise desperately needed funds for the school. This was no small task, because the most popular music of the day was minstrel music, which had white musicians performing skits, music, and dance done up in black-face to mimic Black musicians.

In contrast to the rollicking antics of the black-faced minstrels, The Fisk Jubilee Singers, as they were soon calling themselves, did not tell jokes or dress in the out-landish costumes of the minstrels. Instead, they put on serious performances dressed

The Fisk Jubilee Singers

in formal attire. As such, they were the first exposure that many Northern audiences had to religious music of former slaves. As the group continued to tour, their fame spread and at one concert it was noted that "men threw their hats in the air and shouted "Jubilees! The Jubilees forever!" The group went on to perform for the crowned heads of England, Germany, and Switzerland. After seven years of touring, The Fisk Jubilee Singers had earned some $150,000 for Fisk University, which was no small change in those days! The group continued to perform well into the twentieth century, and in 1902 they had the honor of being among the first Black musicians to record. They waxed the first version ever recorded of "Swing Low Sweet Chariot" on December 1, 1909.

Take Me in the Lifeboat

Key of G

A bluegrass gospel favorite since it was deftly recorded by Flatt and Scruggs, the first recording was by Wade Mainer and Zeke Morris in Atlanta, Georgia on August 6, 1935. I recently had a phone conversation with Wade Mainer, who had just turned ninety-nine years old, who said, "When we were in the studio with the band and all, they suggested that "Take Me in Your Life-boat" would be a nice flip side for "Maple on the Hill." Each song helped one another out, you know. I heard later that Mr. Southern took and got it copyrighted and I couldn't do anything about it, after he'd done

Wade Mainer & Sons of the Mountaineers

done that. Back then, we didn't hardly know what things like that [copyright] was. We didn't know the ropes on the music, so we let it go." According to Gus Meade in his book *Country Music Sources*, "Take Me in a Lifeboat" appeared in a 1882 songbook with credit to J. Courtney. The lyrics and melody, below are from *Old Songs Hymnal*, with lyrics collected by Dorothy G. Bolton, and music arranged by Harry T. Burleigh, 1929. In their version there seems to be a line missing on verse two below.

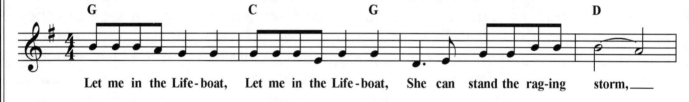

Let me in the Life-boat, Let me in the Life-boat, She can stand the rag-ing storm,___

Let me in the Life-boat, Let me in the Life-boat, she will bear my spir-it home.___

Storms are heavy, winds are loud,
Thunder is rolling and busting in the clouds;
Father and mother are crying say,
Lord Jesus' going to take us in the Life-boat. (Chorus)

Pull for the shore, Sailor,
And don't you fall asleep,
Or you sink on the deep;
Hope in the anchor and this you must keep,
If you want to sit with Jesus in the Life-boat. (Chorus)

Some is at the helm
And some is down below,
The ship is a dashing
And the deck is overflow;
See every Sailor standing at this post
Waiting for the order for the Life-boat. (Chorus)

Take Up Thy Cross

Rev. A. H. Achley   Key of G   Rev. A. H. Achley

Composed in 1922, "Take Up Thy Cross" appeared the same year in *Rodeheaver's Gospel Songs: for Church, Sunday School and Evangelistic Services*. It's been recorded by The Blue Sky Boys, The Stanley Brothers, The Louvin Brothers, J.D. Sumner, Molly O'Day, The Wilburn Brothers, Traditional Grass, and Little Jimmie Dickens. Note this early photo of Little Jimmie Dickens when he was "little."

I walked one day a-long a coun-try road, And there a stran-ger jour-neyed too,

Bent low be-neath the bur-den of His load: It was a cross, a cross I knew.

Chorus

"Take up thy cross and fol-low me." I hear the bless-ed Sav-ior call;

How can I make a les-ser sac-ri-fice, when Je-sus gave His all?

I cried, "Lord Jesus," and He spoke my name;
I saw His hands all bruised and torn;
I stooped to kiss away the marks of shame,
The shame for me that He had borne. (Chorus)

"O let me bear Thy cross, dear Lord," I cried
And, lo, a cross for me appeared,
The one forgotten I had cast aside,
The one, so long, that I had feared. (Chorus)

My cross I'll carry till the crown appears,
The way I journey soon will end
Where God Himself shall wipe away all tears,
And friend hold fellowship with friend. (Chorus)

Tell Mother I Will Meet Her

Ralph S. Tinsman   Key of D   Ralph S. Tinsman

Written around 1900 during the heyday of Tin Pan Alley, this little known sentimental classic was first recorded by Ernest V. Stoneman & His Dixie Mountaineers on January 28, 1927. It was later recorded by a number of North Carolina musicians including Zeke Morris, J.E. Mainer's Mountaineers and Whitey & Hogan.

In a far and dis - tant ci - ty, Dy - ing at the close of day, 'Twas a

fair hair'd boy who'd wan - dered far from home, Take this mess-age to my moth-er

When my work on earth is thro', Tell her that her boy will meet her,

In the land be-yond the blue. Tell my moth - er I will
                                            Tell my moth -er,

meet her   When my work of love and la - bor all is thro',
I will meet her,

Where the good of earth are gath - ered with the faith - ful and the true.

146

Tell Mother I Will Meet Her

In a far and distant city, dying at the close of day,
'Twas a fair haired boy who wandered far from home,
Take this message to my mother when my work on earth is through,
Tell her that her boy will meet her, in the land beyond the blue.

   Tell my mother I will meet her
   When my work of love and labor all is through,
   Where the good of earth are gathered with the faithful and the true,
   Tell her that her boy will met her in the land beyond the blue.

In his hand he held a picture of the old home far away,
In the other 'twas a mother old and gray,
While in accents low he whispered, she will know that I was true,
Tell her that her boy will meet her, in the land beyond the blue. (Chorus)

'Tis my last good-night he whispered, angels gather 'round my bed,
Soon with all my friends and loved ones I shall be
Down the valley of the shadow, Jesus leads me safely through,
Tell her that her boy will meet her, In the land beyond the blue. (Chorus)

To the old home came a message, twas to mother from her boy,
But alas for her the message came too late,
For that day the angels took her, to the faithful and the true,
And tonight she dwells with Willie in the land beyond the blue. (Chorus)

There Is No Hiding Place Down There

Key of G

This old time gospel favorite was first collected in 1907 and published in 1915 in John W. Work's book, *Folk Songs of the American Negro*. Its fame spread when it was recorded by The Carter Family in Camden, New Jersey, on December 11, 1934. Bluegrass fans took notice of the song when it was recorded by Lester Flatt, Earl Scruggs and The Foggy Mountain Boys. This version is from *Old Songs Hymnal*, with lyrics collected by Dorothy G. Bolton, and music arranged by Harry T. Burleigh, 1929.

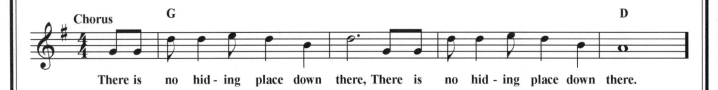

Chorus — *G* — *D*

There is no hid-ing place down there, There is no hid-ing place down there.

Verse — *G*

Went to the rocks to hide my face, The rocks cried out no

D — *G*

hid-ing place! There is no hid-ing place down there.

Rocks cried out, I'm a melting too, (two times)
I want to go to heaven as well as you,
And there's no hiding place down there.

Sinner man he gamble, gamble, and he fell, (3 times)
But wanted to git to heaven,
But he had to go to hell,
And there is no hiding place down here.

The Devil say, I'm a pleading too, (3 times)
I got to have, if I heav [sic] to have you,
And there is no hiding place down there.

Lester Flatt & Earl Scruggs

Twilight Is Falling

A.S. Kieffer   Key of G   B.C. Unseld

Originally entitled "Twilight Is Falling," this song often goes by the title, "Twilight Is Stealing." Like "Grave on the Green Hillside," the lyrics were composed by Aldine S. Kieffer and the melody by Benjamin C. Unseld in about 1878. Both men were important pioneers of American gospel music. The first recording of this song, as "Twilight Is Stealing," was by Dykes' Magic City Trio on March 9, 1927.

Twi- light is steal - ing   o - ver the sea,   Shad - ows are fall - ing   dark on the lea;

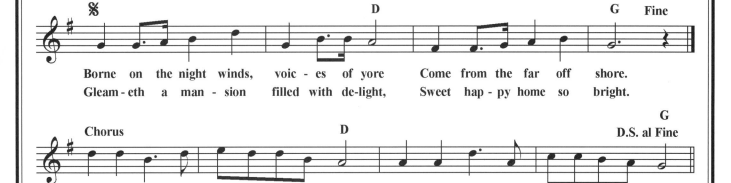

Borne on the night winds,   voic - es of yore   Come from the far   off   shore.
Gleam - eth a man - sion   filled with de - light,   Sweet hap - py home so   bright.

Far a - way be - yond the star - lit skies,   Where the love - light nev - er nev - er dies,

Photo by Wayne Erbsen

Voices of loved ones, songs of the past,
Still linger 'round me while life shall last.
Lonely I wander, sadly I roam,
Seeking that far off home. (Chorus)

Come in the twilight, come, come to me,
Bringing some message from over the sea,
Cheering my pathway while here I roam,
Seeking that far off home. (Chorus)

The Unclouded Day

Rev. J. K. Alwood   Key of G   Rev. J. K. Alwood

Rev. J. K. Alwood was a circuit riding preacher who traveled on horseback to churches in Ohio. He wrote "The Unclouded Day" in 1890 while riding his horse through a long night's journey home. It was first recorded by The Old Southern Sacred Singers in New York City on May 5, 1927.

Oh, they tell me of a home far be - yond the skies, Oh, they

tell me of a home far a - way, Oh, they tell me of a home where no

storm - clouds rise, Oh, they tell me of an un-cloud-ed day.

Oh, the land of cloud - less day, Oh, the land of an un - cloud - ed sky;

Oh, they tell me of a home where my friends have gone,
Oh, they tell me of that land far away,
Where the tree of life in eternal bloom,
Sheds its fragrance through the unclouded day. (Chorus)

Oh, they tell me of a King in His beauty there,
And they tell me that mine eyes shall behold,
Where He sits on the throne that is whiter than snow,
In the city that is made of gold. (Chorus)

Oh, they tell me that He smiles on His children there,
And His smile drives their sorrows away,
And they tell me that no tears ever come again,
In that lovely land of unclouded day. (Chorus)

Walk in Jerusalem Just Like John

Key of G

This old Black spiritual was first recorded as "I Want to Be Ready," on February 14, 1918, by the Tuskegee Institute Singers on RCA Victor. The exact origin of the song may never be known, but it appeared in William E. Barton's 1899 book, *Old Plantation Hymns.* The last verse, a "floater," was first printed as part of the song "Swing Low, Sweet Chariot," which was published in the 1874 book *Hampton Cabin and Plantation Songs.* Bill Monroe, who recorded it for Decca on July 18, 1952, remembered learning it from a Black preacher in Norwood, North Carolina, many years before.

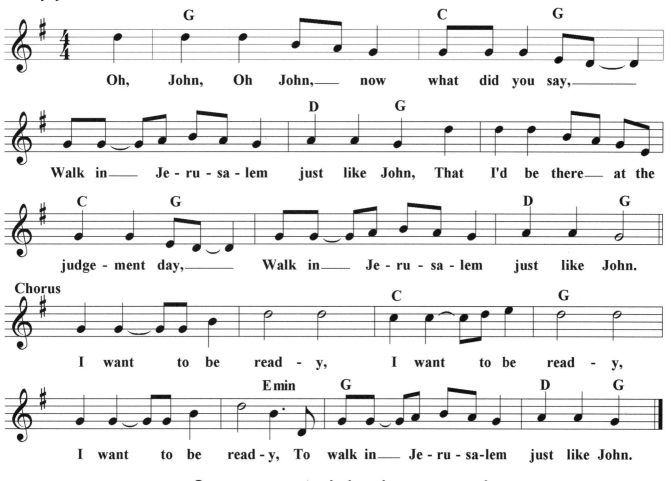

Oh, John, Oh John,—— now what did you say,——

Walk in—— Je-ru-sa-lem just like John, That I'd be there—— at the

judge-ment day,——— Walk in—— Je-ru-sa-lem just like John.

Chorus

I want to be read-y, I want to be read-y,

I want to be read-y, To walk in—— Je-ru-sa-lem just like John.

Some come crippled and some come lame,
Walk in Jerusalem just like John,
Some come walking in Jesus' name,
Walk in Jerusalem just like John. (Chorus)

He lifted the cross upon his shoulder,
Walk in Jerusalem just like John,
I'll meet you there the first crossover
Walk in Jerusalem just like John. (Chorus)

If you get there before I do,
Walk in Jerusalem just like John,
Tell all my friends I'm a-coming too,
Walk in Jerusalem just like John. (Chorus)

Warfare

Key of Am

I first learned this spooky religious song from the singing of E.C. Ball from Rugby, Virginia, from the LP "High Atmosphere" (Rounder 0028). It is still available on the recording "E.C. Ball and Ora Through the Years 1937-1975" (CCCD-0141). The song has been recorded by Ginny Hawker as "My Warfare Will Soon Be Over" on her 2001 CD "Letters from My Father" (Rounder 0491-2). Hawker recently mentioned that she learned the song from Bill & Wilma Milsaps, who live in the Snowbird community near Robbinsville, North Carolina. "Warfare" has recently been recorded by an all-female band with the unlikely name of Uncle Earl. The verse and the chorus use the same melody.

Chorus

My war-fare'll soon be end-ed, My race is near-ly run,

My war-far'll soon be end-ed And I am go-ing home.___

My Lord told his disciples,
After I'm risen and gone,
You will meet with troubles and trials,
But by your rebukes I am strong. (Chorus)

You can rebuke me all you want to,
I'm traveling home to God,
I'm well acquainted with the crossing,
And all our ways are gone. (Chorus)

God bless them Holiness people,
The Presbyterians too,
The good old shouting Methodists,
And the praying Baptists too. (Chorus)

And when I get to heaven,
I want you to be there too,
And when I say "Amen"
I want you to say so too. (Chorus)

Morehead, Kentucky, August, 1940

We Are Going Down the Valley

Jessie Brown Pounds   Key of D   J.H. Fillmore

We are go-ing down the val-ley one by one, With our fa-ces toward the set-ting of the sun, Down the val-ley where the mourn-ful cy-press grows, where the stream of death in si-lence on-ward flows.

Chorus

We are go-ing down the val-ley, Go-ing down the val-ley, Go-ing toward the set-ting of the sun, We are go-ing down the val-ley, Go-ing down the val-ley, go-ing down the val-ley one by one.

We are going down the valley one by one,
When the labors of the weary day are done,
One by one, the cares of earth for ever past,
We shall stand upon the river brink at last. (Chorus)

We are going down the valley one by one,
Human comrade you or I will there have none,
But a tender hand will guide us lest we fall,
Christ is going down the valley with us all. (Chorus)

We Shall Meet Someday

Tillit S. Teddlie   Key of G   Tillit S. Teddlie

How our hearts ache with grief as we say good-bye, We shall

meet some day, Where no sor-row or tears ev-er

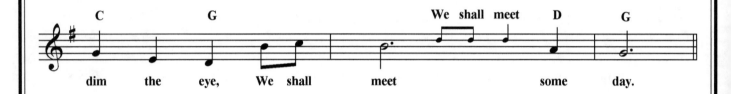

dim the eye, We shall meet some day.

Chorus
We shall meet where no storm clouds gath-er, We shall

meet some day, By the ri-ver of life, spark-ling

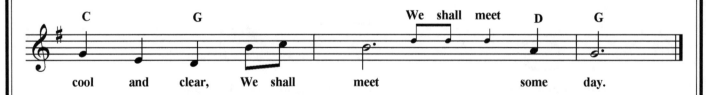

cool and clear, We shall meet some day.

When we've all crossed the stream with its rolling tide,
We shall meet (we shall meet) some day,
In that city of rest on the other side,
We shall meet (we shall meet) someday. (Chorus)

What a glorious thought, as we say good bye,
We shall meet (we shall meet) some day,
In that beautiful home that's prepared on high,
We shall meet (we shall meet) someday. (Chorus)

We'll Understand It Better By and By

Charles A. Tindley   Key of G   1905   Charles A. Tindley

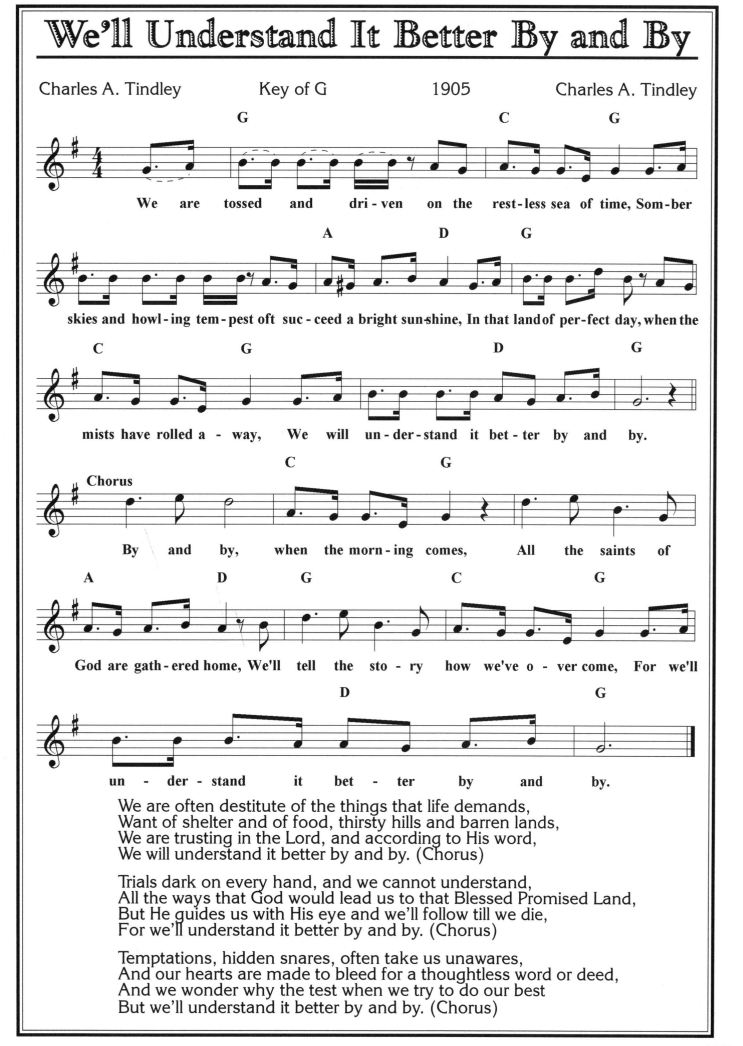

We are tossed and dri-ven on the rest-less sea of time, Som-ber skies and howl-ing tem-pest oft suc-ceed a bright sun-shine, In that land of per-fect day, when the mists have rolled a-way, We will un-der-stand it bet-ter by and by.

Chorus

By and by, when the morn-ing comes, All the saints of God are gath-ered home, We'll tell the sto-ry how we've o-ver come, For we'll un-der-stand it bet-ter by and by.

We are often destitute of the things that life demands,
Want of shelter and of food, thirsty hills and barren lands,
We are trusting in the Lord, and according to His word,
We will understand it better by and by. (Chorus)

Trials dark on every hand, and we cannot understand,
All the ways that God would lead us to that Blessed Promised Land,
But He guides us with His eye and we'll follow till we die,
For we'll understand it better by and by. (Chorus)

Temptations, hidden snares, often take us unawares,
And our hearts are made to bleed for a thoughtless word or deed,
And we wonder why the test when we try to do our best
But we'll understand it better by and by. (Chorus)

What Would You Give in Exchange?

F.J. Berry   Key of G   1912   J.H. Carr

Brother a - far from the Savior to - day,
Risking your soul for the things that de - cay,
O if to - day God should call it a - way,
What would you give in ex - change for your soul?
What would you give in ex - change for your soul?

Chorus

What would you give? in ex - change What would you give? in ex - change
what would you give in ex - change for your soul?
O if to - day God should call it a - way,

Mercy is calling you, won't you give heed?   More than the silver and gold of the earth,
Must the dear Savior still tenderly plead   More than all jewels thy spirit is worth,
Risk not your soul, it is precious indeed   God the creator has given it birth,
What would you give in exchange for your soul?   What would you give in exchange for your soul?

When I Laid My Burdens Down

Key of G

The melody of this old Black spiritual may have been the inspiration for the melody the Carter Family used for their classic recording of "Will The Circle Be Unbroken." This version of "When I Laid My Burdens Down" was collected in Georgia by Dorothy G. Bolton for her book, *Old Songs Hymnal*, published in 1929. Artists who have recorded it include Ernest Phipps and His Holiness Quartet (7/26/1927), The Carter Family (6/07/1938), and Roy Acuff and His Smoky Mountain Boys (4/11/1940).

Rise up mourn - er, rise and tell, When I laid this bur - den down.__ Je - sus

done made all things well, When I laid my bur - den down.

Chorus

Glo - ry Hal - le - lu - jah! When I laid this bur - den down,__

Glo - ry Hal - le - lu - jah! When I laid this bur - den down.

Mind, my sister, how you walk on the cross,
When I laid this burden down,
Your foot might slip and soul be lost,
When I laid my burden down. (Chorus)

My Lord done just what he said,
When I laid my burden down,
He healed the sick and raised the dead,
When I laid my burden down. (Chorus)

When the Roll Is Called Up Yonder

J.M. Black — Key of G — 1893 — J.M. Black

When the trum-pet of the Lord shall sound and time shall be no more, And the

morn-ing breaks, e - ter - nal, bright and fair, When the saved of earth shall ga-ther ov - er

on the oth - er shore, And the roll is called up yon - der, I'll be there.

Chorus

When the roll is called up yon - der, When the

roll is called up yon - der When the roll is called up

yon - der, When the roll is called up yon - der I'll be there.

On that bright and cloudless morning, when the dead in Christ shall rise,
And the glory of His resurrection share,
When His chosen ones shall gather to their home beyond the skies,
And the roll is called up yonder, I'll be there. (Chorus)

Let us labor for the Master from the dawn till setting sun,
Let us talk of all His wondrous love and care,
Then, when all of life is over, and our work on earth is done,
And the roll is called up yonder, I'll be there. (Chorus)

When the Savior Reached Down for Me

G.E. Wright   Key of C   1921   G.E. Wright

Once my soul was a-stray from the heav-en-ly way, And was wretch-ed and vile as could be; But my Sav-ior in love gave me peace from a-bove When He reached down His hand for me. for me

Chorus
When my Sav-ior reached down for me, for me, When my Sav-ior reached down for me; for me; I was lost and un-done, with-out God or His Son, When my Sav-ior reached down for me. for me.

I was near to despair when He came to me there,
And He showed me that I could be free;
Then He lifted my feet, gave me gladness complete,
When He reached down His hand for me. (Chorus)

How my heart does rejoice when I hear His sweet voice,
In the tempest to Him I then flee,
There to lean on His arms, safe, secure from all harm,
When He reached down His hand for me. (Chorus)

159

When They Ring the Golden Bells

Dion De Marbelle   Key of D   1887   Dion De Marbelle

When they finished making Dion DeMarbell they must have thrown away the mold because he was one of a kind. Born in Seville, France, on July 4, 1818, he sailed the seas on a whaling ship, served in the U.S. Navy in the Mexican War of 1847, fought with the Sixth Michigan Infantry in the Civil War, worked as a clown in Barnum & Bailey's first circus, joined Buffalo Bill Cody's Wild West Show and, last but not least, sang in a Methodist church choir.

There's a   land be-yond the riv - er, That we   call the sweet for-ev-er, And we

on - ly reach that shore by faith's de - cree, One by one we'll gain the por-tals, There to

dwell with the   im-mor-tals, When they ring the gol-den bells for you and me.
yond the shin - ing riv - er, When they ring the gol-den bells for you and me.

Chorus

Don't you   hear the bells now ring-ing? Don't you hear the an - gels sing-ing? 'Tis the

glo - ry hal - le - lu - ja Ju - bi - lee, In that far off sweet for-ev - er, Just be -

We shall know no sin or sorrow, in that haven of tomorrow,
When our barque shall sail beyond the silver sea;
We shall only know the blessing of our Father's sweet caressing,
When they ring the golden bells for you and me. (Chorus)

When our days shall know their number, and in death we sweetly slumber,
When the King commands the spirit to be free,
Nevermore with anguish laden we shall reach that lovely aiden,
When they ring the golden bells for you and me. (Chorus)

Where the Soul Never Dies

William M. Golden   Key of G   1914   William M. Golden

Although biographical information about William M. Golden is scarce, we do know he composed a number of classic gospel songs including "A Beautiful Life," and "Oh! Those Tombs." Artists who have recorded "Where the Soul Never Dies" include The Blue Sky Boys, Johnny Cash, The Stanley Brothers, Arthur Smith and His Carolina Crackerjacks, Jim & Jesse, Ricky Skaggs & Tony Rice, and Hank Williams. It is best sung as a duet.

A rose is blooming there for me,
Where the soul (of man) never dies.
And I will spend eternity,
Where the soul (of man) never dies.

A love light beams across the foam,
Where the soul (of man) never dies.
It shines to light the shores of home,
Where the soul (of man) never dies.

My life will end in deathless sleep,
Where the soul (of man) never dies.
And everlasting joys I'll reap,
Where the soul (of man) never dies.

I'm on my way to that fair land,
Where the soul (of man) never dies.
Where there will be no parting hand,
Where the soul (of man) never dies.

Where We'll Never Grow Old

James C. Moore   Key of D   1923   James C. Moore

I have heard of a land on a far a-way strand, 'Tis a
beau-ti-ful home of the soul,——— Built by Je-sus on high, there we
nev-er shall die, 'Tis a land where we ne-ver grow old.

Chorus

Ne - ver grow old, Ne - ver grow old, In a
land where we'll ne-ver grow old, Ne - ver grow old,
Ne - ver grow old, In a land where we ne-ver grow old.

In that beautiful home where we'll nevermore roam,
We shall be in the sweet by and by,
Happy praise to the King through eternity sing,
'Tis a land where we never shall die. (Chorus)

When our work here is done and the life-crown is won,
And our troubles and trials are o'er,
All our sorrow will end, and our voices will blend,
With the loved ones who've gone on before. (Chorus)

While recording this song in 1994, I discovered that two of the singers in the quartet, Bucky Hanks (tenor) and Steve Taylor (bass), were both related to the composer!

Who Will Sing For Me?

J.T. Ely   Key of G   J.T. Ely

Made famous by Ralph and Carter Stanley and by Flatt and Scruggs, "Who Will Sing For Me?" is a bluegrass gospel classic. Here is the original melody and lyrics as first published in 1922.

"Written in memory of Vallie Shipley who departed this life November 21st, 1918."

Oft I sing for my friends when death's cold form I see,

But when I am called will some one sing for me. (for me,)

Chorus
I won - der who will sing for me When I'm
(I won-der who, will sing for me,)

called to cross the si-lent sea, Who will sing for me.
(who will sing for me, for me.)

Where the voice of my King shall call me home above,
Oh, who then will sing the parting song for me. (Chorus)

But I know that at last with our life's record fair,
With trials all past, we all shall sing up there. (Chorus)

So I'll sing till the end and helpful try to be,
Assured that some friend will sing a song for me. (Chorus)

The Stanley Brothers

163

Will the Circle Be Unbroken?

Ada R. Habershon   Key of G   Chas. H. Gabriel

When anyone mentions "Will the Circle Be Unbroken," they are invariably referring to the song made popular by The Carter Family. In New York City on May 6, 1935, the Carters recorded a song they called "Can the Circle Be Unbroken." They apparently took part of the melody and the chorus from song "Will the Circle Be Unbroken," and added their own verses about the death of their mother. Here, finally, is the original song that was taken from *Alexander's Gospel Songs*, New York, 1908. Among the artists who recorded the original version were The Monroe Brothers and The Morris Brothers.

There are loved ones in the glo - ry Whose dear forms you oft - en miss,

When you close your earth - ly sto - ry Will you join them in their bliss?

Chorus

Will the cir - cle be un - brok - en By and by, by and by?

Is a bet - ter home a - wait - ing In the sky, in the sky?

In the joyous days of childhood,
Oft they told of wondrous love
Pointed to the dying Saviour,
Now they dwell with Him above. (Chorus)

You can picture happy gatherings,
'Round the fireside long ago,
And you think of tearful partings,
When they left you here below. (Chorus)

You remember songs of heaven,
Which you sang with childish voice,
Do you love the hymns they taught you,
Or are songs of earth your choice? (Chorus)

One by one their seats were emptied,
One by one they went away,
Now the family is parted,
Will it be complete one day? (Chorus)

164

Will There Be Any Stars?

E.E. Hewitt　　　　Key of G　　　　1897　　　　John R. Sweney

I am think-ing to-day of that beau-ti-ful land, I shall reach when the sun go-eth down, When thro' won-der-ful grace by my Sav-ior I stand, Will there be an-y stars in my crown?

Chorus

Will there be an-y stars, an-y stars in my crown, When at eve-ning the sun go-eth down? When I wake with the blessed in the man-sions of rest, Will there be an-y stars in my crown?

In the strength of the Lord let me labor and pray,
Let me watch as a winner of souls,
That bright stars may be mine in the glorious day,
When His praise like a sea billow rolls. (Chorus)

Oh, what joy it will be when His face I behold,
Living gems at His feet to lay down,
It would sweeten my bliss in the city of gold,
Should there be any stars in my crown. (Chorus)

165

Wondrous Love

Key of Dm

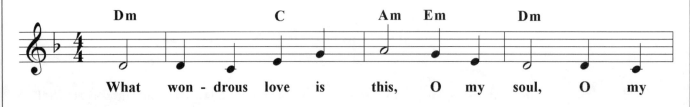

What won - drous love is this, O my soul, O my

soul, What won - drous love is this, O my soul,

What won - drous love is this, that caused the Lord of

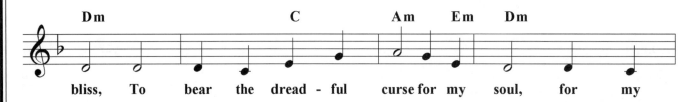

bliss, To bear the dread - ful curse for my soul, for my

soul, To bear the dread - ful curse for my soul.

When I was sinking down, sinking down, sinking down,
When I was sinking down, sinking down,
When I was sinking down, beneath God's righteous frown,
Christ laid aside His crown for my soul, for my soul,
Christ laid aside His crown for my soul.

To God and to the Lamb I will sing, I will sing,
To God and to the Lamb I will sing,
To God and to the Lamb, who is the great "I Am,"
While millions join the theme I will sing, I will sing,
While millions join the theme, I will sing.

And when from death I'm free, I'll sing on, I'll sing on,
And when from death I'm free, I'll sing on,
And when from death I'm free, I'll sing and joyful be,
And through eternity I'll sing on, I'll sing on,
And through eternity I'll sing on.

Photo by Wayne Erbsen

Won't You Come and Sing For Me?

Key of G

Hazel Dickens is one of the greatest singers of traditional, original, and bluegrass songs. Here are Hazel's own words about the origins of this song. "I wrote 'Won't You Come and Sing For Me' in the mid 'sixties as a tribute to a people, a place and a time tucked away forever in my early childhood memories. There was a deep sense of humility, a love and kindness that guided these kindred spirits and bonded these common people. Their old style of singing, their old Primitive songs have surely left their imprints on my singing style and much of my writing. One of my fondest memories is being surrounded by the sheer raw vocal power of the whole congregation singing unaccompanied in unison, unleashing all that pent up raw emotion in the notes of a song. It is a sound that could only come from whence it came."

Hazel Dickens

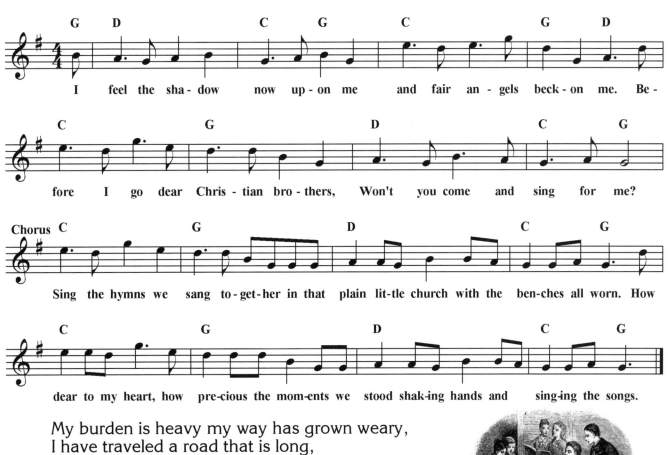

I feel the sha-dow now up-on me and fair an-gels beck-on me. Be-fore I go dear Chris-tian bro-thers, Won't you come and sing for me?

Chorus Sing the hymns we sang to-get-her in that plain lit-tle church with the ben-ches all worn. How dear to my heart, how pre-cious the mom-ents we stood shak-ing hands and sing-ing the songs.

My burden is heavy my way has grown weary,
I have traveled a road that is long,
And it would warm this old heart, my brother
If you'd come and sing one song. (Chorus)

In my home beyond that dark river,
Your dear faces no more I'll see,
Until we meet where there's no more sad partings
Won't you come and sing for me?

Working on a Building

Key of G

After receiving numerous requests for this song, Bill Monroe learned it from the Carter Family's version recorded on May 8, 1934. On January 25, 1954, Bill Monroe recorded it as a duet with Jimmy Martin, who sang lead on the chorus. This version of "Working on a Building" was collected in Georgia in the late 1920s by Dorothy G. Bolton as "I Work on a Building Too." It was published in her book *Old Songs Hymnal* in 1929. Only the last verse and the chorus resemble the more common lyrics that are sung nowadays. It is interesting to note that the musical phrasing on the chorus seems to have an almost Calypso feel. Although this version was collected in Georgia, it is entirely possible that it originated even further south.

Photo by Wayne Erbsen

If I was a li-ar, I tell you what I would do,

I'd lay down all my ly-ing ways And go work on a build-ing too.

Chorus
I'm work-ing on a build-ing for my Lord, For my Lord,

For my Lord, I'm work-ing on the build-ing for my Lord, I'm work-ing on the build-ing too.

If I was a underminer, I tell you what I would do,
I would lay down all my undermining ways
And go work on the building too. (Chorus)

If I was a sinner, I tell you what I would do,
I would lay down all my sinning ways
And go work on the building too. (Chorus)

If I was a peacebroker, I tell you what I would do,
I would lay down all my peacebroking ways
And go work on the building too. (Chorus)

Index of Songs

A Beautiful Life 24
A Picture From Life's Other Side 26
Ain't Gonna Lay My Armor Down 28
Amazing Grace 29
Angel Band 30
Are You Washed in the Blood? 31
Beautiful 32
Church in the Wildwood 34
Come and Dine 35
Come Thou Fount 36
Crying Holy Unto My Lord 37
Daniel Prayed 38
Death Is Only a Dream 40
Deep Settled Peace 42
Diamonds in the Rough 44
Don't You Hear Jerusalem Moan? 46
Drifting Too Far From the Shore 48
From Jerusalem to Jericho 50
Give Me the Roses Now 52
Glory-land Way, The 53
Good Old Way, The 54
Grave on a Green Hillside 56
Hallelujah Side, The 58
Hallelujah, We Shall Rise 60
Hand in Hand With Jesus 61
He Will Set Your Fields on Fire 62
Heaven Above 64
Hold Fast to the Right 66
Hold to God's Unchanging Hand 68
Home in That Rock 70
How Beautiful Heaven Must Be 72
I Am a Pilgrim 74
I Am Bound For the Promised Land 75
I Feel Like Traveling On 76
I Have Found the Way 77
I Heard My Mother Call My Name in Prayer 78
I Will Never Turn Back 80
I Would Not Be Denied 81
If I Could Hear My Mother Pray Again 82
I'll Be No Stranger There 84
I'm Going That Way 86
I'm Going Through 88
I'm S-A-V-E-D 90

Index of Songs

In the Garden 92
In the Sweet By and By 94
I've Just Seen the Rock of Ages 95
Jesus, Savior, Pilot Me 96
Just a Closer Walk With Thee 97
Just One Way to the Gate 98
Just Over in the Gloryland 100
Keep on the Sunny Side of Life 101
Kneel at the Cross 102
Leaning on the Everlasting Arms 104
Let the Church Go Rolling On 105
Let the Lower Lights Be Burning 106
Life's Railway to Heaven 107
Little Moses 108
Lone Pilgrim, The 110
Lord, I'm Coming Home 111
Methodist Pie 112
My Old Cottage Home 114
Oh! Those Tombs 115
Old Account Was Settled, The 116
Old Gospel Ship, The 118
Old Rugged Cross, The 120
Old-Time Religion 122
On the Sea of Life 124
On the Sunny Side of Life 126
Our Meeting is Over 127
Palms of Victory 128
Pass Me Not 130
Pilgrim of Sorrow 132
Poor Wayfaring Stranger 133
Power in the Blood 134
Precious Memories 135
Row Us Over the Tide 136
Royal Telephone, The 137
Shake Hands With Mother Again 138
Shall We Gather at the River? 139
Standing in the Need of Prayer 140
Swing Low Sweet Chariot 142
Take Me in the Lifeboat 144
Take Up Thy Cross 145
Tell Mother I Will Meet Her 146
There Is No Hiding Place Down There 148
Twilight Is Falling 149
Unclouded Day, The 150

Index of Songs

Walk in Jerusalem Just Like John 151
Warfare 152
We Are Going Down the Valley 153
We Shall Meet Someday 154
We'll Understand It Better By and By 155
What Would You Give in Exchange? 156
When I Laid My Burdens Down 157
When the Roll Is Called Up Yonder 158
When the Savior Reached Down for Me 159
When They Ring Those Golden Bells 160
Where the Soul Never Dies 161
Where We'll Never Grow Old 162
Who Will Sing For Me? 163
Will the Circle Be Unbroken? 164
Will There Be Any Stars? 165
Wondrous Love 166
Won't You Come and Sing For Me? 167
Working on a Building 168

Native Ground Books & Music

BOOKS OF SONGS, INSTRUCTION & HOME COOKING

1st American Cookie Lady
A Garden Supper Tonight!
Aunt Barb's Bread Book
Backpocket Bluegrass Songbook
Backpocket Old-Time Songbook
Bluegrass Banjo For Ignoramuses!
Bluegrass Mandolin for Ignoramuses!
Children at the Hearth
Clawhammer Banjo For Ignoramuses!
Cowboy Songs, Jokes, Lingo 'n Lore
Fiddle For Complete Ignoramuses!
Flatpicking Guitar for Ignoramuses!
Front Porch Songs, Jokes & Stories
Hymns of the Old Camp Ground
Log Cabin Cooking
Log Cabin Pioneers

Lost Art of Pie Making
Mama's in the Kitchen
Old-Time Farmhouse Cooking
Old-Time Gospel Songbook
Outhouse Papers, The
Outlaw Ballads, Legends, & Lore
Railroad Fever
Rousing Songs of the Civil War
Secrets of the Great Old-Timey Cooks
Singing Rails
Southern Mountain Banjo
Southern Mountain Mandolin
Southern Mountain Fiddle
Southern Mountain Guitar
Southern Mountain Dulcimer
Take Two & Butter 'Em

RECORDINGS

An Old-Fashioned Wingding
Ballads & Songs of the Civil War
Battlefield Ballads of the Civil War
Cowboy Songs of the Wild Frontier
Front Porch Favorites
Log Cabin Songs
Love Songs of the Civil War
The Home Front

Old-Time Gospel Instrumentals
Railroadin' Classics
Railroad Fever
Rural Roots of Bluegrass
Singing Rails
Songs of the Santa Fe Trail
Southern Mountain Classics
Southern Soldier Boy

OLD-TIME GOSPEL FAVORITES
by Wayne Erbsen
is a great CD of thirteen of the songs in this book

Write or call for a FREE catalog
Native Ground Books & Music
109 Bell Road
Asheville, NC 28805 (800) 752-2656
banjo@nativeground.com
www.nativeground.com